Assessment Practices
in
Foreign Language Education
DIMENSION 2004

Lynne McClendon
Rosalie M. Cheatham
Denise Egéa-Kuehne
Carol Wilkerson
Judith H. Schomber
Jana Sandarg
Scott T. Grubbs
Victoria Rodrigo
Miguel Mantero
Sharron Gray Abernethy

Editors
C. Maurice Cherry
Furman University

Lee Bradley
Valdosta State University

Selected Proceedings of the 2004 Joint Conference of the
Southern Conference on Language Teaching
and the Alabama Association of Foreign Language Teachers

SCOLT Publications
1165 University Center
Valdosta State University
Valdosta, GA 31698
Telephone 229 333 7358
Fax 229 333 7389
http://www.valdosta.edu/scolt/
Lbradley@valdosta.edu

ISBN 1-883640-17-2

Valdosta State University provided equipment and facilities
in support of the work of
preparing this volume for press.

TABLE OF CONTENTS

Review and Acceptance Procedures
SCOLT *Dimension*

The procedures through which articles are reviewed and accepted for publication in the proceedings volume of the Southern Conference on Language Teaching (SCOLT) begin with the submission of a proposal to present a session at the SCOLT Annual Conference. Once the members of the Program Committee have made their selections, the editors invite each presenter to submit the abstract of an article that might be suitable for publication in *Dimension*, the annual volume of conference proceedings.

Only those persons who present *in person* at the annual Joint Conference are eligible to have written versions of their presentations included in *Dimension*. Those whose abstracts are accepted receive copies of publication guidelines, which follow almost entirely the fifth edition of the *Publication Manual of the American Psychological Association*. The names and academic affiliations of the authors and information identifying schools and colleges cited in articles are removed from the manuscripts, and at least four members of the Editorial Board and the co-editors review each of them. Reviewers, all of whom are professionals committed to second language education, make one of four recommendations: publish as is, publish with minor revisions, publish with significant rewriting, or do not publish.

The editors review the recommendations and notify all authors as to whether their articles will be printed. As a result of these review procedures, at least three individuals decide whether to include an oral presentation in the annual conference, and at least six others read and evaluate each article that appears in *Dimension*.

2004 SCOLT Editorial Board

Introduction

One of the most onerous, yet critical tasks facing members of the Board of Directors of the Southern Conference on Language Teaching (SCOLT) is that of selecting a theme well in advance of each annual conference. Given the current climate of demands for accountability and reform at national, state, and local levels in both K-12 and post-secondary institutions, "Assessment Practices in Foreign Language Education" seemed particularly timely as the theme for the 2004 SCOLT meeting, March 18-20, in Mobile, Alabama. Although the invitation for presenters to submit abstracts for articles to be considered for publication clearly stated that authors were not required to address this topic, each of the contributions most highly recommended by our Editorial Board for inclusion in this volume dealt with the theme, either in part or almost exclusively.

Before readers begin perusing the eight primary articles in this collection, the editors urge them to pay special attention to the announcement on pp. xi-xv, where Lynne McClendon and Carol Wilkerson introduce a new series of articles on assessment, to include an annotated bibliography on the subject in the 2005 volume of *Dimension*. The authors also provide an overview of the two agencies approved to accredit teacher education programs–the National Council for Accreditation of Teacher Education (NCATE) and the Teacher Education Accreditation Council (TEAC)–and explain how certification requirements, teacher licensure, and mandatory tests vary across the states in the SCOLT region.

Touted at its inception as a major educational policy reform at the national level and hailed by many as a much-needed initiative to mandate the kind of change required to diminish many of the inequities in public education and hold states, districts, and even individual schools accountable for the failure of their students to demonstrate sufficient progress, the No Child Left Behind Act of 2001 (NCLB) quickly became a political football. The legislation attracted intense criticism once results of high-stakes testing and other criteria used as evidence of success or failure showed that many schools and districts were not making the grade in terms of mandated progress goals, often because of the obvious inconsistencies in establishing similar goals for otherwise comparable schools and districts. Nevertheless, NCLB is a reality, and individual teachers, schools, and districts currently have little recourse but to make every effort to comply with both the spirit and the letter of the law. In "No Child Left Behind in Foreign Language Education," Lynne McClendon provides an overview of the law as it affects second language (L2) teachers. More specifically, though, she examines in detail one of the key phrases in the legislation, "highly qualified teachers," as it is defined by the law, explores ways in which current and aspiring L2 teachers and their administrators and supervisors can assess progress being made towards meeting the goals of the NCLB act, and suggests ways in which they can ensure that they are complying with the law in a timely fashion.

Academic territoriality, parochial interests, and, on occasion, sheer paranoia often lead to the maintenance of a curricular status quo in higher education, thereby resulting in total stagnation of course offerings and program development. Despite the fact that L2 programs at numerous colleges and universities have made considerable progress in having their courses reflect the latest philosophies concerning L2 acquisition, the transformation of the overall curriculum design of a particular department or program in many cases shows little evidence of change over a period of two or more decades. In "Using Learner and Teacher Preparation Standards to Reform a Language Major," Rosalie Cheatham explores the ways in which a foreign language department at one large university assessed its need for reform and overhauled its curriculum to bring it more closely in line with current best practices, with attention to existing L2 standards and the specific needs of those enrolled in teacher education programs.

Portfolio review has become a mainstay of assessment tools at many educational levels. In "Student Electronic Portfolio Assessment," Denise Egéa-Kuehne provides an overview of the terminology related to assessment and discusses some of the ways in which program assessment and evaluation have been practiced with varying degrees of success in recent years. The author then cites both advantages and limitations of using the electronic portfolio as a mechanism for assessing the progress of individual students. Of particular value to those interested in undertaking a similar venture is the concrete information the author provides concerning both the organization of such a program and the specific list of technological tools essential to the successful implementation of electronic portfolio assessment.

Few experiences prove so disheartening to an aspiring teacher as that of completing a prescribed program of course work and perhaps even a teaching internship, only to receive a score falling below the established minimum on a mandatory standardized test. Just when such would-be teachers see themselves as being on the threshold of beginning a career in L2 education, they see their dreams shattered. One of the issues of greatest concern to those preparing teachers for qualifying exams is the inconsistency among states in terms of both the specific tests being required and the discrepancies in cutoff scores from one state to another. Of equal concern is the nature of the specific exams in terms of content and delivery of questions. In "Assessing Readiness of Foreign Language Education Majors to Take the Praxis II Exam," Carol Wilkerson, Judith Schomber, and Jana Sandarg survey such inequities and concerns and offer concrete recommendations as to how candidates for certification can best prepare themselves to achieve acceptable test scores.

"Total Physical Response" has become such a staple in the vocabulary of L2 educators that it is most commonly simply referred to as "TPR," and the term "Total Physical Response Storytelling" (TPRS) has more recently become almost as widely known. Long an integral component of language programs in elementary schools, TPR has in recent years been integrated into the curricula of language classes for more mature learners. Nevertheless, the use of TPR both as a component of the overall assessment process for individual language development and as a measure of programmatic success has to date received insufficient recognition, as Scott Grubbs reminds readers in "The TPR Test: Total Physical Response as an Assessment Tool." The author further argues convincingly that in addition to being an effective pedagogical vehicle during early language instruction and a viable evaluation instrument, TPR can be used to appeal to the multiple intelligences of a diverse population of language learners.

A survey of the majority of methods texts and bibliographies of articles on L2 education reveals that the amount of literature on listening comprehension in L2 education generally pales in comparison to that available on the speaking, reading, and writing skills. Therefore, any contribution in the area of developing listening skills is particularly welcome if it adds something fresh, as is the case in Victoria Rodrigo's "Assessing the Impact of Narrow Listening: Students' Perceptions and Performance." After surveying previous findings concerning the role of listening in L2 learning, the author defines "narrow listening" (NL), provides a framework for the systematic integration of NL into the L2 curriculum, and shares guidelines for the development of the audio library critical to the success of the NL approach. Finally, the author provides positive results from an assessment of both students' perceptions of the approach and the effects of NL on their actual listening skills, as measured by an aural comprehension test.

In "Accounting for Activity: Cognition and Oral Proficiency Assessment," Miguel Mantero examines another of the basic L2 skills, speaking, both with reference to the specific ways in which cognition plays a role in the assessment of speaking proficiency, according to the *ACTFL Proficiency Guidelines,* and with respect to determining the degree to which cognition should be a fundamental part of any assessment of oral proficiency. Through a meticulous analysis of several oral proficiency interviews and collaboration with an external evaluator solicited to provide an objective point of view, the author concludes that cognition must occupy a more central role in assessment of speaking proficiency and recommends that classroom instructors make use of *instructional conversations* and a framework of *indigenous assessment criteria* to enhance the abilities of their students to demonstrate greater overall proficiency.

Because prospective employers and admissions committees continue to raise their expectations of job applicants and candidates for admission to graduate programs and professional schools, college students make increasing demands on their institutions to provide a more extensive range of internships, as is particularly the case for those eager to integrate their interests in business and L2 study. In "Building Bridges for International Internships," Sharron Abernethy details the structure of one university's language/business internship program, describes the procedure by which it was assessed, and in several appendices shares both a syllabus and a number of forms that may prove useful as models for those interested in developing similar programs at their institutions.

We believe that L2 professionals at all levels will view this volume as a diverse collection of informative articles, but we hope that readers will find them truly enjoyable as well.

The Editors

Lee Bradley
Valdosta State University
Valdosta, GA

Maurice Cherry
Furman University
Greenville, SC

Acknowledgments

Among our greatest pleasures in preparing each volume of *Dimension* is that of working with an Editorial Board as generous with its time as it is knowledgeable about the field of second language education. We continue to recruit reviewers from within and beyond our SCOLT region, teachers of various languages at the elementary level, in graduate schools, and at every stage in between. This year's 19 readers hail from 16 different states and include those familiar with a broad range of critical issues in second language education, research problems, legal concerns, and a vast array of contemporary methodologies and instructional techniques. Our reviewers are attentive to detail, and, in addition to their predictable role in citing both the strengths and weaknesses of specific articles, many share with those whose articles are to be published invaluable advice concerning potential references that might otherwise have been overlooked, questions that should be addressed, and recommendations for clarification of language or a change in focus in the treatment of a particular subject.

It should go without saying that the authors deserve our praise as well, because they have been willing to heed the advice of the reviewers, accepting most suggestions in a positive way and in a few cases convincingly defending their original observations. Even in the final days of our preparation of this volume, the editors have had to communicate with almost all of the authors, in some cases requesting clarification of a specific term or phrase and in others asking for a last-minute update of a Web address or bibliographical reference. In every case the authors have responded promptly and courteously.

Because many of those teaching second languages are less familiar with the APA style than with other manuscript formats and since technological advances have made citations of electronic references fairly complex, the task of double-checking Web sources for accuracy and that of cross-checking text citations against the References section of each article at times prove tedious. We therefore owe special thanks to Donté Stewart, a Furman University undergraduate who has assisted with the proofreading and verification of the many references in these articles.

As always, the editors of *Dimension* and the SCOLT Board of Directors owe our greatest debt to the Administration of Valdosta State University for having made available to us the resources necessary for publication of this volume. Without such support, *Dimension 2004* would not exist in its present state.

Lee Bradley and
C. Maurice Cherry, Editors

Announcement:

Special Series on Assessment

Lynne McClendon
Executive Director
Southern Conference on Language Teaching

Carol Wilkerson
Carson-Newman College

On the eve of its 40th anniversary, the Southern Conference on Language Teaching (SCOLT) plans a special series of articles on assessment within the foreign language profession. The 2004 edition of *Dimension* offers an overview of the instruments used to evaluate teacher education programs that prepare foreign language teacher candidates and examines the teacher evaluation instruments required for licensure in the SCOLT region. The series will continue in the 2005 edition of *Dimension* with an annotated bibliography of noteworthy and recommended articles on assessment.

Accreditation of Teacher Education Programs: NCATE and TEAC

There are two teacher education accrediting agencies approved by the U.S. Department of Education. The National Council for Accreditation of Teacher Education (NCATE) was founded in 1954 and was acknowledged as the only agency responsible for accrediting teacher education programs in 1992. Over 500 institutions have met NCATE accreditation standards, and 48 states have a partnership with NCATE to conduct joint or concurrent reviews. The Teacher Education Accreditation Council (TEAC) was founded in 1997 and recently received federal acknowledgement as an accrediting agency by U.S. Secretary of Education Rod Paige. There are currently three institutions that have undergone TEAC review and several others in the review process. The difference between these two agencies can be seen in their distinct approaches in verifying the validity of a teacher education program and its ability to deliver knowledgeable and skilled P-12 teachers.

NCATE is a performance-based accreditation system. A paper review of an institution's teacher education program is conducted either by the state or by a foreign language professional organization according to the agreement NCATE has with the state of the institution making application for accreditation. A Board of Examiners conducts an on-site visit to evaluate the capacity of the program to meet standards of delivery. The following standards form the basis of the NCATE review:

I. Candidate Performance
    Standard 1: Candidate knowledge, skills, and dispositions
    Standard 2: Assessment system and unit evaluation

II. Unit Capacity
    Standard 3: Field Experiences and Clinical Practice
    Standard 4: Diversity
    Standard 5: Faculty Qualifications, Performance, and Development
    Standard 6: Unit Governance and Resources

After submitting the *Intent to Seek NCATE Accreditation* form and meeting obligations required for this process, institutional programs seeking NCATE accreditation must provide a program report no longer than 140 pages with a cover letter, an overview section, response to the standards to be met, and appendices with supporting documentation. The American Council on the Teaching of Foreign Languages (ACTFL) partnered with NCATE to develop the specific foreign language standards, using the rubrics "approaches standard," "meets standard," and "exceeds standard" to qualify the applicant's degree of meeting them. After a review of the information submitted with the Board of Examiners' report, NCATE awards one of the following designations: *first accreditation, provisional accreditation, continuing accreditation, conditional accreditation,* or *accreditation with probation.* Those interested in further information regarding the accreditation process, should access the NCATE Web site at <http://www.ncate.org>.

The heart of the TEAC process is based on the examination of student learning and on the quality of evidence submitted by an institution to support its claim that students are meeting established learning objectives. Each component also has a focus on learning how to learn, multicultural perspectives and accuracy, and technology. The following represent TEAC's goals and principles:

Quality Principle I
    1.0   Evidence of Student Learning
    1.1   Subject matter knowledge
    1.2   Pedagogical knowledge
    1.3   Teaching skill

Quality Principle II
    2.0   Valid Assessment of Student Learning
    2.1   Evidence of links between assessments and the program goal, claims, and requirements
    2.2   Evidence of valid interpretations of assessment

Quality Principle III
    3.0   Institutional Learning
    3.1   Program decisions and planning based on evidence
    3.2   Influential quality control system

Standards of Capacity for Program Quality
  4.1   Curriculum
  4.2   Faculty
  4.3   Facilities, Equipment, and Supplies
  4.4   Fiscal and Administrative
  4.5   Student Support Services
  4.6   Recruiting and Admissions Practices, Academic Calendars, Catalogs, and Publications
  4.7   Student Complaints

A major component of the TEAC process involves the *Inquiry Brief* prepared by the institution undergoing evaluation. This academic piece must describe clear and evaluative goals for student learning and the application of these goals in curriculum design and pedagogy, evidence of student learning, the way in which the institution allows for continuous improvement, and the strength of the seven capacity standards. TEAC sends trained auditors to the institution to conduct the site visit through a thorough investigation of the *Inquiry Brief*, including a request for raw data to verify the claims made in this document. During the audit visit, the institution has the opportunity to update important changes that may have taken place since the submission of the *Inquiry Brief*. The audit team turns over its completed audit report to the Accreditation Panel to allow evaluation of the evidence in order to determine which of the following categories of accreditation will be awarded to the institution: *accreditation, new program* or *pre-accreditation, provisional accreditation,* or *denied accreditation.* For further information regarding the TEAC accreditation process and schools that have undergone this process, access the web site at <http://www.teac.org>.

Teacher Evaluation Instruments in the SCOLT Region

The 13 states that comprise the Southern Conference on Language Teaching (SCOLT) differ in the languages for which they certify teachers and in their certification requirements. To simplify matters, the discussion that follows examines certification instruments for French, German, and Spanish. However, Web sites are provided for the benefit of readers wishing information for other modern languages and the classics.

In the SCOLT region all states except Alabama, Florida, and Texas require teacher candidates to take the *Praxis II Exam* for licensure to teach French, German, or Spanish. The *Praxis II Exam* is a series of exams developed and administered by Educational Testing Service (ETS), a professional test development company based in Princeton, New Jersey. State departments of education or agencies responsible for licensing specify which of the various component tests in the Praxis Series will be used for certification, and they establish their state's minimum passing scores.

The two most commonly required component tests are the Productive Language Skills Test and the Content Knowledge Test. The Productive Language Skills Test is a 2-hour test of candidates' speaking and writing abilities. The Content Knowledge Test is a 2-hour test of 120 multiple-choice questions, divided into four sections. The first section evaluates interpretative listening; the second tests knowledge of the structure of the target language; the third assesses interpretative reading; and the fourth tests knowledge of cultural perspectives. Test-takers respond to questions about language and culture based upon tape-recorded listening passages and printed material. Details about specific tests, languages not mentioned above, and passing scores may be found at <www.ets.org/praxis/prxstate.html>.

Licensure in Alabama, Florida, and Texas

Three states in the SCOLT region have their own, distinct licensure requirements. In Alabama, teacher candidates take a common basic skills test, but each college or university designs its own comprehensive content exam for licensure. This procedure may change, as a U.S. District Court mandate allows that in 2005 the state may resume implementing subject matter testing (J. Meyer, personal communication, October 28, 2003).

Candidates in Florida take state-made, multiple-choice and essay tests for their content areas. The Spanish test assesses candidates' proficiency in speaking, listening, writing, and reading, as well as their knowledge of Hispanic cultures (of both Spain and Spanish America), language structure, and principles of second language acquisition.

The French test assesses candidates' communication skills, their knowledge of French and Francophone cultures, and their knowledge derived from French and Francophone sources and their connections with other disciplines and information. In addition, the test evaluates candidates' knowledge of pedagogy and their knowledge of the nature of language and culture through comparisons of French and their own language and culture.

The German test references the 1986 *Proficiency Guidelines* of the American Council on the Teaching of Foreign Languages to assess candidates' comprehension at an advanced level of spoken German passages pertaining to different times and places on topics of general interest and daily routine and their ability to converse in German at an intermediate-high level, to write German at an intermediate-high level, and to read at an advanced level a simple connected German passage dealing with a variety of basic personal and social needs and topics of general interest. In addition, the test assesses the examinees' knowledge of the following: basic German vocabulary in areas of general interest and application of vocabulary skills, basic German grammar and syntax in context, the social customs and daily life of German-speaking countries, the history and geography of German-speaking countries, arts and sciences, and pedagogy and professional knowledge. More information and details about language not mentioned may be found at <www.fldoe.org/edcert>.

Teacher candidates in Texas take the locally developed multiple-choice *Examination for the Certification of Educators in Texas* (*ExCET*) for certification in French, German, and Spanish. However, Texas is in the midst of replacing the *ExCET* tests with the *Texas Examination of Educator Standards* (*TExES*), reported to be based on public school curriculum (State Board for Educator Certification Information and Support Center, personal communication, October 28, 2003). The *TExES* exams contain five subareas that assess listening, written communication, language structures, vocabulary and usage, and language and culture. Details about the *TExES* may be found at <www.texes.nesinc.com>. French and Spanish candidates are also required to take the *Texas Oral Proficiency Test* (*TOPT*), a 75-minute test in which candidates record their responses to a total of 15 picture, topic, and situational tasks that range from intermediate to superior levels of proficiency. A thorough description of each *TOPT* test is available at <www.topt.nesinc.com>.

Given the mobility of contemporary society, readers interested in transferability of certification should examine reciprocity agreements established by The National Association of State Directors of Teacher Education and Certification (NASDTEC). Such information is available at <www.nasdtec.org>.

1

No Child Left Behind
in Foreign Language Education

Lynne McClendon
SCOLT Executive Director

Abstract

> The No Child Left Behind (NCLB) Act of 2001, the revised Elementary and Secondary Education Act, is one of the most sweeping educational reform movements in recent times. While there are many subcomponents of this Act, one area specifically touches on foreign language education: "highly qualified teachers." This article examines the term "highly qualified teacher" as defined by NCLB, as well as effective practices highly qualified foreign language teachers, curriculum program specialists, and college of education instructors can employ to leave no child behind in foreign language education. Using this information, teachers, curriculum program specialists, and college of education instructors can evaluate their own progress and programs to ensure that all students achieve a level of success in foreign language studies.

Background

Leaving no child behind implies that *all* students can learn. Over the last decade and a half, foreign language education has been shaped by a guiding "can-do" philosophy reflected in the American Council on the Teaching of Foreign Languages (ACTFL) Statement of Philosophy in *Standards for Foreign Language Learning in the 21st Century*:

> Language and communication are at the heart of the human experience. The United States must educate students who are equipped linguistically and culturally to communicate successfully in a pluralistic American society and abroad. This imperative envisions a future in which ALL students will develop and maintain proficiency in English and at least one other language, modern or classical. (National Standards in Foreign Language Education Project, 1999, p. 7)

This same commitment is echoed in the publication *World Languages Other Than English Standards* (National Board for Professional Teaching Standards, 2001): "Accomplished teachers are dedicated to making knowledge accessible to all students. They act on the belief that all students can learn" (p. vi).

States receiving Title I funding must ensure that the teachers of the "core academic subjects"–English, reading or language arts, mathematics, science, *foreign languages*, civics and government, economics, arts, history and geography–meet the definition of "highly qualified" to continue receiving funding (No Child Left Behind Act of 2001, 2002). The term "highly qualified," according to the National Governors Association article, "NCLB: Teacher Quality Legislation," indicates "that the teacher has obtained full state certification (including alternative certification) or passed the state teacher licensing examination, and holds a license to teach in such state" (2002). The article declares that new elementary teachers, in addition to having obtained state certification at the minimum of the bachelor's level, must also have "passed a test of knowledge and teaching skills in reading, writing, mathematics, and other areas of the basic elementary school curriculum." Likewise new middle and high school teachers, in addition to holding a valid state certificate at the bachelor's level, must also "have demonstrated competency in each of the teacher's subjects."

Regarding veteran teachers, Title IX, section 9101 (23) (C), stipulates that these teachers must also hold a valid certificate at the bachelor's level and meet the same standards required of new teachers by completing course work, passing a test, or by demonstrating competence in all subject matter taught by the teacher. The timeline for accomplishing the "highly qualified" teacher status for *all* teachers in the core subjects, including foreign language, is by the end of the 2005-2006 school year. As of 2002-2003, states and local educational agencies must begin reporting progress toward this goal and ensuring that "new hires" have met the standards set forth.

Prospective foreign language teachers at the undergraduate levels would do well to work with their institutions' departments of education to ensure they have the appropriate coursework and are prepared as well for teacher tests or other means of accountability. Beyond the teacher tests, it is important for modern foreign language teachers to be fluent enough to use language as a means of instruction in the classroom. Many colleges and universities offer study-abroad programs designed to enhance basic language skills obtained in the classroom. As post-secondary departments of education begin aligning their courses of study with the National Council for Accreditation of Teacher Education (NCATE)[1] standards and guidelines, the prospective foreign language teacher will be on track for successfully passing tests that may be required by the state as a part of the licensure process and for performing successfully in the classroom as well.

NCATE was founded in 1954 as a nonprofit and nongovernmental organization devoted to the pursuit of ensuring quality teacher education programs through rigorous standards that the education departments of universities and colleges must meet in order to become NCATE-accredited. Several educational organizations and associations comprise the NCATE council and contribute to the ongoing research and refinement of what constitutes effective teacher education programs. There is an established process for applying for accreditation, with preconditions for being accepted as a candidate, a program review inclusive of both review of the portfolio and an on-site review, follow-up reports, and maintenance of accreditation once an educational unit has obtained its first accreditation. NCATE also provides workshops for institutions interested in initiating the process.

What are these standards that NCATE has indicated as the foundations of good teacher preparation programs, and how were they created? The basic NCATE standards, developed by teacher educators, practicing teachers, content specialists, and local and state policy-makers, were based on researched practices and conditions for learning. Various content-related organizations and groups working with NCATE took the next step of ensuring usable standards by addressing the core standards in terms of the particular content area. In this respect ACTFL played an important role in defining the standards in terms of foreign language education. Using research from the field, the ACTFL Standards Writing Team set forth six content standards that in general address the following categories: (1) proficiency in the target language, (2) recognition of the role of culture and incorporating other disciplines, (3) language acquisition theories and practices, (4) standards-based curriculum and implementation of standards in daily lesson plans, (5) the importance of varied assessments as an integral part of instruction, and (6) the importance of professional growth for self-improvement with the ultimate goal of providing the best instruction and classroom environment for all students.

In turn, these six content standards contain subsets of standards, supporting explanations, and rubrics by which education programs can determine the extent to which they are preparing future foreign language teachers. The rubric measure terms (*Approaches Standard, Meets Standard, and Exceeds Standard*) are particularly helpful in determining where program fine-tuning may be needed, and it is this information that can be particularly instructive to foreign language curriculum supervisors and practicing foreign language teachers. Since many of the new teachers will be entering the teaching field with NCATE preparation, the current teaching field would do well to use these rubrics to self-assess and make determinations regarding what professional development is needed. Such self-assessments based on these rubrics could support a curriculum specialist in designing or requesting funding for professional development opportunities. In this way the foreign language classroom becomes a receptive and continuous improvement environment, edifying for newly certified teachers, current teachers, and most of all, the students. These six content standards add another dimension to the term "highly qualified" teachers.

Obviously, "highly qualified" teachers should possess good teaching skills, but what are "good teaching skills"? A definition of these goals, not a part of the original bill as it was first introduced in the House, was added to H.R. 2211 (engrossed as agreed by the House) "Ready to Teach Act of 2003, Teacher Quality Enhancement Grants, section 201" to provide some insight into what some legislators considered to constitute "good teaching skills," described as follows:

(9) TEACHING SKILLS: The term "teaching skills" means skills that
    (A) are based on scientifically based research;
    (B) enable teachers to effectively convey and explain subject
        matter content;

(C) lead to increased student academic achievement; and
(D) use strategies that
  (i) are specific to subject matter;
  (ii) include ongoing assessment of student learning;
  (iii) focus on identification and tailoring of academic instruction to students's [*sic*] specific learning needs; and
  (iv) focus on classroom management.

What models are available for foreign language teachers to evaluate their personal performance in relation to defining "good teaching"? The National Board certification process sponsored by the National Board for Professional Teaching Standards (NBPTS)[2] presents a wonderful opportunity for teachers, particularly veteran teachers, to hone their skills and advance student learning. Teachers both in their portfolio and the one-day assessment center activities are evaluated on 14 standards. The NBPTS publication, *World Languages Other Than English Standards* (2001), produced by the National Board for Professional Teaching Standards, provides elaboration of these standards and asks prospective candidates to reflect upon how they are currently meeting these foreign language standards and perhaps to consider some steps to take to address perceived deficiencies. The following titles from the table of content represent the 14 standards:

Knowledge of Students, Fairness, Knowledge of Language, Knowledge of Culture, Knowledge of Language Acquisition, Multiple Paths to Learning, Articulation of Curriculum and Instruction, Learning Environment, Instructional Resources, Assessment, Reflection as Professional Growth, Schools/Families and Communities, Professional Community, and Advocacy for Education in World Languages Other Than English

While some states and local school systems may offer either financial assistance or salary incentives for those undertaking this certification process, teachers can at least self-assess their own standing regarding the standards presented in this document whether or not they pursue the certification. Castor (2002) of NBPTS says, "I routinely heard from participating teachers that the process of seeking this unique credential was the best form of professional development they had ever experienced, because it forced them to re-examine and rethink their teaching." Of course, many foreign language teachers are already addressing these standards and would want to pursue obtaining the certification.

These standards, closely related to those found in the NCATE materials, provide an excellent measure for all foreign language teachers. It should be noted that among the committee members who developed the standards are past and present ACTFL Executive Council members as well as other noted foreign language educators. Many language organizations are offering assistance with the certification process or facets of the process that will enable teachers to be successful participants and, of course, "highly qualified." The NBPTS website[2] lists the foreign language teachers who are designated as "National Board Certified Teachers."

Another document, *Model Standards for Licensing Beginning Foreign Language Teachers: A Resource for State Dialogue*, produced by the Interstate New Teacher Assessment and Support Consortium (INTASC)[3] and sponsored by the Council of Chief State School Officers, addresses similar standards found in the NCATE and NBPTS documents. Likewise, the INTASC standards exist in many content areas. The committee charged with developing the INTASC foreign language standards correlated the 10 basic INTASC core principles to the performance expectations for a foreign language teacher. As a result, the following titles represent the standards for evaluation of effective foreign language teaching:

> Content Knowledge, Learner Development, Diversity of Learners, Instructional Strategies, Learning Environment, Communication, Planning for Instruction, Assessment, Reflective Practice and Professional Development, and Community

Additional information found in the "standards context" provides teachers with an in-depth understanding of each standard and yet another opportunity to self-assess.

The purpose of the INTASC document is to provide direction for setting policies pertaining to licensure, program approval, and professional development of quality foreign language teachers. While this consortium was created in 1987, the addition of the foreign language component is as recent as 2001-2002, when the committee was formed and work was initiated on the foreign language standards. ACTFL and many of the language specific organizations played a major role in helping to shape the INTASC foreign language standards in line with research-based effective practices. Other committee members included practicing teachers of foreign language education, teacher educators, school leaders, and state educational agency personnel. As state educational agencies begin to address the issue of "highly qualified" teachers and ensuring that "no child is left behind," they will doubtlessly rely upon this document already supported by state superintendents or chief school officers. INTASC is already in the process of creating a test that will assess a beginning teacher's knowledge of pedagogical practices and a set of performance assessments for new teachers to show that a teacher can design, implement, and evaluate lessons for diverse learners. Teachers, supervisors of foreign language teachers, colleges of education, and foreign language organizations would do well to review these standards as a means of designing activities and programs for helping teachers obtain the "highly qualified" designation.

Finally, for the K-12 teachers who want to focus primarily on instruction and student evaluation to ensure that they are using the best practices to leave no child behind, the *ACTFL Performance Guidelines for K-12 Learners* (1998), provide a barometer for how well students should be performing at the novice, intermediate, and pre-advanced stages. These guidelines are grounded in the *Standards for Foreign Language Learning in the 21st Century* (NSFLEP, 1999), which define what the K-12 foreign language curriculum should look like. Furthermore, these guidelines are arranged by modes of communication: *interpersonal* (face-to-face communication, as well as personal letters and e-mail), *interpretive* (one-way reading or listening), and *presentational* (one-way writing and speaking). Within these modes, language descriptors are provided for *comprehensibility, comprehension, language control, vocabulary, cultural awareness,* and *communication strategies.* The following example shows the progression of one guideline for "Comprehensibility/Interpersonal" across the three stages.

Comprehensibility (How well are they understood?)/ Interpersonal

Novice Learners	**Intermediate Learners**	**Pre-Advanced Learners**
Rely primarily on memorized phrases and short sentences during highly predictable interactions on very familiar topics ...	Express their own thoughts using sentences and strings of sentences when interacting on familiar topics in present time ...	Narrate and describe using connected sentences and paragraphs in present and other time frames when interacting on topics of personal, school and community interests ...

Reproduced with permission from the American Council on the Teaching of Foreign Languages.

Using the guidelines chart from which the above sample is taken, teachers can easily identify the stage for a particular group of students and further identify the number of descriptors their students can satisfactorily complete. By so doing, teachers have the opportunity to plan instruction for the students who are not performing at the level suggested by the descriptors. The performance chart lists student characteristics and behaviors that can serve as benchmarks for noting student progress in demonstrating language proficiency. It is also important to note that the National Assessment on Educational Progress (NAEP) test in foreign language (Spanish), scheduled for administration in 2004, uses the following tasks to evaluate student skills: interpretive listening and reading, interpersonal listening and speaking, and presentational writing.

Conclusion

The National Association of State Boards of Education (NASBE), speaking through its recent publication, the *Complete Curriculum: Ensuring a Place for the Arts and Foreign Languages in America's Schools* (2003), considers "highly qualified teachers" important enough to list steps to be taken in its first 3 of 10 recommendations to ensure that foreign languages and the arts remain strong and viable subjects of study. As noted by Tesser and Abbott (2003), a core group of dedicated foreign language professionals, with input from the wider language and educational community, has helped to develop consistent themes, measures, expectations, and philosophical underpinnings to the documents mentioned in this discussion. The language profession is the better for this unified approach because it offers sound research-based and agreed-upon directions for what constitutes foreign language teacher quality. The issue of defining a "highly qualified" teacher is perplexing, and, as Berry (2002) suggests, it will definitely not be productive if federal guidelines focus primarily on subject matter competence. Nonetheless, the foreign language profession is indeed very fortunate to have many well-crafted collaborating models of what goes into making teachers "highly qualified" and, in the final analysis, what will produce more fluent users of foreign languages.

Notes

[1]   More detailed information regarding the application process, workshops and timeline for the first accreditation and standards can be located at the NCATE Web site: <www.ncate.org>.

[2]   Information on becoming National Board Certified can be obtained at the NBPTS Web site: <www.nbpts.org>.

[3]   Information regarding INTASC and for ordering a bound copy of the *Foreign Language Standards* document can be located at the Web site for the Council of Chief State School Officers: <www.ccsso.org>.

References

American Council on the Teaching of Foreign Languages (ACTFL). (1998). *ACTFL performance guidelines for K-12 learners* (with fold-out Assessment Chart). Yonkers, NY: author.

Berry, B. (October 2002). *What it means to be a "highly qualified teacher."* Southeast Center for Teacher Quality. Retrieved January 4, 2004, from http://www.teachingquality.org/resources/pdfs/definingHQ.pdf

Castor, B. (2002). Better assessment for better teaching. *Education Week, 22,* 28-30.

National Association of State Boards of Education (NASBE). (2003). *The complete curriculum: Ensuring a place for the arts and foreign languages in America's schools.* Alexandria, VA: NASBE.

National Board for Professional Teaching Standards (NBPTS). (2001). *World languages other than English standards (for teachers of students ages 3-18+).* Arlington, VA: NBPTS.

National Governors Association. (2002, July 26). *NCLB: Summary of teacher quality legislation.* Retrieved January 4, 2004, http://www.nga.org/center/divisions/1,1188,C_ISSUE_Brief^D_4163,00.html

National Standards in Foreign Language Education Project. (1999). *Standards for foreign language learning in the 21st century.* Yonkers, NY: ACTFL.

No Child Left Behind Act of 2001. Office of Elementary and Secondary Education. (2002). (H.R. 1, 107th Cong. (2001), P.L. 107-110). Student Achievement and School Accountability Conference (October 2002). Slide 12. http://www.ed.gov/admins/tchrqual/learn/hqt/edlite-slide012.html

Ready to Teach Act of 2003. (H.R. 2211, 108th Cong. 2003; engrossed). Retrieved January 4, 2004, from http://thomas.loc.gov/cgi-bin/query/D?c108:2:./temp/~c108rd1bvY::

Tesser, C. C., & Abbott, M. (2003). INTASC model foreign language standards for beginning teacher licensing and development. In C. M. Cherry & L. Bradley (Eds.), *Dimension 2003: Models for excellence in second language education* (pp. 65-73). Valdosta, GA: Southern Conference on Language Teaching.

Title IX, 9101(23) "Highly qualified [definition]" (C). Elementary and Secondary Education Act (2002). P.L. 107-110. Retrieved January 4, 2004, http://www.ed.gov/legislation/ESEA02/pg107.html

2

Using Learner and Teacher Preparation Standards to Reform a Language Major

Rosalie M. Cheatham
University of Arkansas at Little Rock

Abstract

While foreign language educators in many university programs have worked to modify courses to reflect the emerging research on the best practices for enabling language acquisition by student learners, the overall curriculum design of language majors remains very similar to structures in place more than two decades ago. This article describes a series of initiatives that have led to a major redesign of a French curriculum at a state university that uses as its organizing principle the two recently developed professional Standards documents: the Standards for Foreign Language Learning in the 21st Century (National Standards in Foreign Language Education Project, 1999) and the ACTFL Program Standards for the Preparation of Foreign Language Teachers (2002).

Background

For over a decade language department faculty at the University of Arkansas at Little Rock have been actively engaged in systematic initiatives to establish meaningful assessment of programs and students reflecting the most current professional research. These efforts have resulted in content revisions in a number of courses in French, German, and Spanish and in the use of oral proficiency interviews and written assessment for all language majors immediately prior to graduation as a measure of program assessment. Since many faculty believe that course grades are the most accurate reflection of a student's language ability, a specific level of mastery has not been requisite to graduation. The syllabi of skill courses have changed substantially over the decades to reflect current understandings of best practices for language instruction, but the overall curricular structure leading to a major or minor has remained remarkably similar to that of decades earlier, when neither proficiency nor standards were bywords of professional language educators.

The current modifications in the French program that have utilized both the Learner Standards K-16, *ACTFL Standards for Foreign Language Learning in the 21st Century* (National Standards in Foreign Language Education Project, 1999) and the recently approved Teacher Standards, *ACTFL Program Standards for the Preparation of Foreign Language Teachers* (2002) as the organizing principle have resulted in the most significant structural change in the curriculum to date. These changes have been specifically designed to assure that all students acquire a more comprehensive and appropriate command of the target language than was common in a more traditional program.

The Challenge

Both language and pedagogy faculty in the department have been actively engaged using federal and state-funded grants in advocating to K-12 foreign language educators throughout the state the appropriate application of the learner standards in their programs. There has, however, been little incentive to effect the changes required to embrace the learner standards in the university curriculum until the recent approval of the American Council on the Teaching of Foreign Languages (ACTFL)/National Council for Accreditation of Teacher Education (NCATE) Teacher Preparation Standards in October 2002. This new impetus results from the fact that Arkansas law requires that an institution of higher education be NCATE-accredited in order for its pre-service teacher candidates to be eligible for licensure. Failure to attain the requisite levels of proficiency by language teacher candidates could, therefore, jeopardize the ability of licensure candidates in all disciplines at the university to obtain teaching credentials. The specific imperative that has led to the curricular reform described below is to assure that licensure candidates in French have the maximum opportunity to attain the skill levels required by the approved Teacher Preparation Standards.

This challenge is exacerbated by two additional realities. One of the requirements for teacher candidates to attain the knowledge, skills, and dispositions described in the *ACTFL Program Standards for the Preparation of Foreign Language Teachers* (2002) is "an ongoing assessment of candidates' oral proficiency and provision of diagnostic feedback to candidates concerning their progress in meeting required levels of proficiency" (p. 24). Additionally, "candidates who teach languages such as French ... must speak at a minimum level of Advanced-Low as defined in the *ACTFL Proficiency Guidelines-Speaking* (1999)" (p. 21). While this level of oral skill is understandably desirable and a reasonable minimum for classroom teachers, it is a significant pedagogical challenge to university students, as most of the program's current graduates begin their study of French at the university level. A decade-long effort to provide the highest quality instruction for all students and recognition of challenges presented by the new Teacher Preparation Standards are evident in the revised curriculum.

The Early Initiatives

Like their colleagues at many other institutions, faculty at UALR have for many years attempted to keep abreast of the most current trends and research initiatives in foreign language pedagogy. Therefore, as proficiency guidelines were first developed and subsequently codified in the 1986 publication of the *American Council on the Teaching of Foreign Languages/ Interagency Language Roundtable (ACTFL/ILR) Proficiency Guidelines,* a documented shift began in the lower-level skill courses toward an attempt to provide instruction that enabled students to communicate in the target language. Modified Oral Proficiency Interviews (MOPI) were required in many language skill courses and students in some academic programs outside the language department were required to attain at least an interview rating of Intermediate-Mid in order to satisfy degree requirements. Although these early efforts were somewhat primitive when compared to the expectations and activities in modern textbooks and the opportunities for skill enhancement embodied in various technological applications hardly envisioned at the time, the change from teaching students about the language to enabling them to communicate in the language has been embraced for years.

The first substantive curricular change occurred in the mid-1980s, when three levels of conversation courses were added to the French program. The major was revised to require all students to complete as a part of their degree requirements at least one three-semester-hour conversation course at the intermediate or advanced level as well as a more traditional stipulation for a course in culture and civilization and at least two courses in literature. The reality, of course, was that apart from the conversation and culture offerings, the only other content available was in the canon of literature courses defined either by century or genre. However, the formal shift to valuing student output of language began at this point.

The next documented institutional effort to update curricular content occurred in 1992, when the entire language department at UALR became actively engaged in the Reforming the Major Project, sponsored by the American Association of Colleges and Universities. Working as a committee of the whole, the foreign language faculty determined that the original *ACTFL Proficiency Guidelines* (1986) should be the organizing principle for skill courses at all levels and, in addition, that all students should be assessed using the common metric of the proficiency guidelines. The faculty in each language worked collaboratively to develop an assessment instrument in each language that included testing of speaking, listening, writing, and reading skills. This assessment was to serve not only as a record of student skill but also as a measure of the effectiveness of course instruction in improving each student's proficiency in each skill. Each student was tracked so that it would be possible to determine the relative success of students who began their study of the language at the university level, as measured against those who had studied over a period of years in K-12 programs or who had studied or lived abroad.

By chance, the assessment decisions that were a result of the Reforming the Major Project coincided with the university-wide implementation of a new language requirement for students pursuing a bachelor of arts degree. This provision required students to complete nine semester hours of a language (specifically six hours at the elementary level and three hours at the intermediate level) or demonstrate equivalent proficiency. Eager to document to what extent, with what rapidity, and in which courses student proficiency increased, initial determinations of the department faculty provided for the newly developed assessment instruments to be used at three points. The first administration was to be near the completion of the nine-semester-hour requirement; the second was a course completion component in the advanced skills sequence required for majors and minors; and finally, the same assessment instrument was administered to students immediately prior to graduation. Although this emphasis on assessment was a well-intentioned effort to document individual student progress and the effectiveness of course sequencing in improving proficiency, it soon became evident that the logistics of administering and grading three assessments per student were a burden, took away from instructional time, and helped neither the overall language acquisition of the student nor provided essential data in the determination of the effectiveness of the course work leading to the major. Performance on the multiple assessments seemed to reflect student interest and effort to demonstrate proficiency as much as it showed real progress in knowledge or ability. The faculty decided, then, to administer the listening, reading, and writing assessment only once, at the end of each student's program of study, and to continue the use of the oral proficiency interview.

The Second-Year Courses

When in 1996 the department faculty became a part of the national Language Mission Project (Maxwell, Johnson, & Sperling, 1999) proficiency-oriented assessment was already requisite for all students majoring in a foreign language, and the faculty had enough experience to be well aware of the limitations of assessment instruments to demonstrate course or program quality. The Language Mission Project provided a new opportunity for department faculty to undertake a collaborative exploration of the purposes and practices of foreign language teaching and learning. Since a significant focus of participation in this project was on assuring that the language curricula reflected the institution's mission and because the language requirement after 4 years was fully operational, department faculty determined to focus on the content of the final "required" course, the third-semester (Intermediate I) course. This decision was made as faculty recognized that many students were taking the third-semester course primarily to complete a requirement, whereas previously most students had enrolled in a third semester either as the first step toward a major or toward a minor. Where the course had previously served as a beginning for serious language study, it had become an ending for a large majority of students.

French faculty made a key decision to substantially alter the course content from the traditional systematic reentry of structures taught in the elementary course sequence toward a serious attempt to organize the syllabus around intermediate-level proficiency guidelines. Believing that students who completed nine semester hours of language study should be able to "do something" with their language and knowing that a one-semester intermediate course was "too short" to assure that students would achieve a sophisticated level of skill mastery, the faculty determined to organize the course around the intermediate-level speaking and writing proficiency guidelines, wherein students are expected to be able to survive in the target culture and to make themselves understood in predictable situations. Tests and quizzes were minimized, and a series of three projects was implemented, each of which was designed around real-world activities and focused on both skills and content that students would need in order to demonstrate culturally appropriate survival skills.

While the exact format of the project emphasis has varied, each relates to survival. Topics include requirements for a successful study abroad experience, for working abroad, or for employment with a local company seeking an employee who can communicate minimally in French. Required activities include having students present themselves to a potential host family by writing a letter of introduction and recording an audio- or videotape on which they talk about themselves for the family or the university abroad and describe their family, hobbies, job, and school interests. Another project option requires students to develop an appropriate *curriculum vitae* for presentation to a company with an opening in its international department for someone with some communicative competence in French. All students must be able to seek basic information in French required to move into an apartment and set up housekeeping or to live with a family in the target culture who do not speak English. Because the language proficiency required for these projects is in the intermediate range, the skills students must demonstrate are both reasonable and appropriate for anyone completing the nine-semester-hour requirement. A major success of the project focus is that students end the course and their required language study with an understanding that they can use French for something relevant. Prior to the implementation of this concept, most students completed the course far more aware of the limitations of their knowledge (as evidenced by errors on tests) than of what they could accomplish.

The other fundamental change that this project focus required was that the choice of structure and grammar to be taught be determined as a derivative of the project content, as opposed to the more common systematic grammar review that most intermediate textbooks provide. For example, students are taught linguistic skills necessary to seek real-world information, as opposed to working on exercises that use all the interrogative adverbs (e.g., "I'm looking for the closest bank," rather than "Where is the closest bank located?"; or "I need to buy a télécarte," instead of "Where should I go to buy a télécarte?"). In an attempt to provide students with authentic and manageable input, the faculty selected texts published by French publishing companies for teaching French as a foreign language. While by no means a perfect solution, the *Café Crème* series (Di Giura & Trevisi, 1998) provided a different format for accessing the needed content than was available in other materials and had the added advantage of being relatively contemporary and inexpensive for a one-semester course requirement.

One significant component of the exercise and assessment items contained in these books is the usage of DELF-style activities (Commission Nationale du DELF et du DALF, 2001). These activities are similar to many situation-based exercises in American texts but tend to utilize more culturally authentic materials and native-level language. While not a direct parallel to the Proficiency Guidelines that are now so fundamental to language instruction in the United States, the competency required for success on the DELF (Diplôme d'Etudes en Langue Française) *premier degré* and *second degré* or even the DALF (Diplôme Approfondi de Langue Française) shares many commonalities with the skill progression reflected in the *Proficiency Guidelines*. Both DELF and DALF are internationally recognized examinations and as such provide external validation to both students and university administrators that the language and skills that students are learning are applicable beyond the borders of the course in which they are enrolled at the university. The intent of DELF and DALF, similar to that of the *ACTFL Proficiency Guidelines*, is to evaluate the know-how of students and not simply their linguistic knowledge independent of its context or usage.

As both levels 2 and 3 of the *Café Crème* texts (DiGiura & Trevisi, 1998) were used in both the intermediate and advanced skills courses, the students became clearly aware that know-how was the goal. This emphasis on know-how and proficiency was again reinforced when the *TFI* (*Test de français international*, 2001) first became available. It is a multiple-choice test designed to assess a student's ability to understand, speak, read, and write French as it is used in the international workplace and in everyday life. The faculty decided to use the *TFI* in lieu of the assessment instrument developed by the department and accompany it with the oral proficiency interview, so that it would be possible to provide students with an internationally recognized assessment of their proficiency in French. This decision changed the role of the required "completion of the major" assessment from a program assessment to a student assessment, but no other curricular modifications occurred. The second semester of the intermediate course continued where the required Intermediate I course ended, followed by a two-semester advanced skills sequence, conversation classes, and relatively traditional culture, civilization, and literature courses. French faculty discussed numerous options for broadening the scope of curricular revisions, but it was not until the standards became the new focus that reform in upper-level courses began to take shape.

The *Standards* and the Curriculum

With the publication of the Learner Standards K-16 in the *Standards for Foreign Language Learning in the 21st Century* (National Standards in Foreign Language Education Project, 1999), a new paradigm emerged in language instruction to reflect the understanding that language acquisition can be appropriate and attainable for all students when it is appropriately focused on what students should know and be able to do. Subsequently, the development of the *ACTFL Program Standards for the Preparation of Foreign Language Teachers* (2002) brought a new imperative to the level of skill acquisition for pre-service teachers. As stated earlier, pre-service teacher preparation is a major issue for programs in Arkansas, as the possibility for all disciplines at the university to have candidates obtain licensure hinges on the demonstrated ability of students in each licensure area to meet or exceed the requirements of their discipline for initial licensure. Many students who continue into upper-level French classes begin their language study at the university level, and few of them begin their study of French with the intent of becoming K-12 teachers. Furthermore, the teacher standards require a demonstration of progress over a period of time. Therefore, the faculty determined to use both the learner and the teacher preparation standards as the guiding principle for the next step in curricular modification, and any revisions would be applicable to all students. As a result, if students who had not previously intended to become licensure candidates decided to do so near the end of their undergraduate academic career, the instruction they would have received and the artifacts that would have been retained would enable them to have the requisite credentials to seek licensure as though such had been their original intent.

The new licensure requirement is that a candidate be able to document progress in skill development over a period of time. Hence, the need to retain artifacts of course work throughout the progression of courses leading to a degree is essential. Since measuring by "standards" in any context should raise the bar on student performance criteria, it was anticipated that making the standards applicable to every student would have the added benefit of improving the proficiency of all students in each skill area.

The focus of instruction shifts away from the teacher as the one who imparts knowledge. The new research referenced in the *ACTFL Program Standards for the Preparation of Foreign Language Teachers* (2002) suggests that "the course work taken in the language major influences how the future teacher conceptualizes what it means to know the target language, culture and literature and most importantly, how the language is taught" (p. 7). Within these *Standards* it is understood that standards 1 and 2 are content standards and deal specifically with the outcomes of the course work in the language classroom. The other standards are more directly connected to the pedagogical skills that pre-service teachers must acquire as part of language pedagogy training and are not directly applicable to the French curriculum modifications detailed here It is clear, however, that if a university program expects its pre-service teachers to meet or exceed the Teacher Preparation Standards and qualify for licensure, it is essential that language departments take seriously the content knowledge required. It is pursuant to this reality that the final stage of curriculum reorganization took place.

What have come to be referred to as the "five *C*s" of the learner standards–Communication, Cultures, Connections, Comparisons and Communities–have become the rubrics for the organization of the French curriculum beyond the initial three-course requirement sequence. Rather than continuing a two-semester intermediate skills sequence, one of which fulfilled the requirement for the bachelor of arts degree, followed by two semesters of advanced skills focusing traditionally on the productive skills of speaking and writing, the second intermediate and both advanced skill courses were modified to reflect the content of the Communication standard. Entitled "Integrated Skills I, II, and III" respectively, each course is independent of the others and focuses on one of the three "communicative modes": interpersonal, interpretive, or presentational.

Clearly much of the content required in these courses is similar to that of earlier iterations of "proficiency-oriented" instruction. However, using the particular mode as the organizing principle assures that it is the student production that is important, while the specific activities or content may vary from semester to semester and from student to student, depending on their individual interests. Newspaper and magazine articles on current events selected from Internet sources may provide the input for students to enhance their ability to understand written French in the interpretive course, while students may develop Web pages or

PowerPoint presentations on a topic discussed in a course from another discipline in the presentational course.

The challenge for faculty is to assure that content and input are appropriate and that the expected productive outcomes can be measured in a way that encourages students to progress. A newer series of texts, *Reflets* (Capelle & Gidon, 2000) is being used for aural input along with *Communication Progressive du Français avec 365 activités* (Miquel, 2003), a series of thematically oriented interpersonal exercises, to support the three-course communicative mode courses.

The next phase of curricular modification focuses on the Cultures, Connections, and Comparisons standards. Under this grouped rubric, there are three culture and civilization courses that emphasize the perspectives, practices, and products that describe the Cultures standard, enabling students to gain knowledge and understanding of Francophone cultures throughout the world (Connections) and compare these behaviors to their own (Comparisons).

Finally, a series of seminars and practica uses a variety of sources to provide the opportunity for content-based study and for acquiring a more profound understanding of linguistic patterns and systems than was contained in the lower-level courses (Comparisons). Up to 12 semester hours of credit may be granted for study abroad, and receiving credit for an internship experience in the target culture is an additional option. Both opportunities give life to the Communities standard within the undergraduate curriculum. The traditional century- and genre-based literature courses have not yet been formally removed from the curriculum, but they are not being offered as the new curriculum design is implemented.

As all of these substantive curricular modifications are phased in, beginning with the 2003-2004 academic year, and as the major is reorganized to reflect the new rubrics, the process is rendered even more significant as the faculty endeavors to accommodate the avowed aim of the *ACTFL Program Standards for the Preparation of Foreign Language Teachers* (2002), which

> are the most recent and thorough attempt to establish clear expectations for teacher preparation and reflect a reconceptualization of foreign language teaching . . . based on the assumption that learning to teach is a long-term, complex, developmental process that starts with competencies in language and culture and operates through participation in the social practices and context associated with learning and teaching. (p. 5)

It is too early to know whether the change in structure of the French major and the focus on learner and teacher standards will result in a significant improvement in the proficiency level in all skills for all students or whether Advanced Low oral proficiency will become a reality for a significant percentage of students. It is, however, already evident that students understand clearly that the opportunities for language acquisition and output are practical, real world, and attainable. This understanding is reflected in both their enthusiasm and in the quality of their performance. Anecdotal and experiential evidence suggests that as enthusiasm for language production and quality of communicative competence increase, overall skill mastery will be demonstrably enhanced.

References

American Council on the Teaching of Foreign Languages. (2002). *ACTFL program standards for the preparation of foreign language teachers.* Yonkers, NY: ACTFL.

American Council on the Teaching of Foreign Languages. (1986). *ACTFL proficiency guidelines.* New York: ACTFL.

American Council on the Teaching of Foreign Languages. (1999). *ACTFL proficiency guidelines–speaking.* New York: ACTFL.

Capelle, G., & Gidon, N. (2000). *Reflets, Méthode de français.* Paris: Hachette.

Commission Nationale du DELF et du DALF, Centre International d'Études Pédagogiques. (2001). *Guide des sujets du DELF et du DALF.* Paris: Didier.

Di Giura, M., & Trevisi, S. (1998). *Café Crème.* Paris: Hachette.

Maxwell, D., Johnson, J. S., & Sperling, J. (1999). Language mission project: A report of findings. *Liberal Education, 85,* 40-47.

Miquel, C. (2003). *Communication progressive du français.* Paris: Clé International.

National Standards in Foreign Language Education Project. (1999). *Standards for foreign language learning in the 21st century.* Yonkers, NY: ACTFL.

Test de français international. (2001). Kingston, ON, Canada: Chauncey Group International.

3

Student Electronic Portfolio Assessment

Denise Egéa-Kuehne
Louisiana State University

Abstract

A brief review of the traditional types of assessment used in second language education is followed by a discussion of the limitations of standardized testing. The author then addresses the challenge of assessing a student's development over time with a performance-based approach, showing how one alternative assessment form, the electronic portfolio, can help teachers keep track of a student's progress over a long period of time and also provide valuable information for curriculum specialists, principals, school boards, parents, and the community. The technologies necessary to support the development of electronic portfolios and its step-by-step procedures are described.

Background

As foreign language educators, we constantly have to test, evaluate, and assess our students. On the basis of these results, we are expected to make informed decisions as to their level of achievement and progression with respect to predetermined norms and criteria, to adjust our instruction accordingly, and to provide information to schools and educational agencies. In 1996, a new educational tool was made available to all members of the profession when the American Council on the Teaching of Foreign Languages published the final draft of the *Standards for Foreign Language Learning in the 21st Century* (National Standards in Foreign Language Education Project). Although the document includes 12 sample progress indicators for grades 4, 8, and 12 that define student progress in meeting the standards, these progress indicators are not performance standards themselves, and it was left up to individual states and school districts to determine performance standards for their students. Besides asking for performance-based assessment, content standards, which indicate what students should know and be able to do, raise the issue of documenting students' increased competency in subject matter and of doing so over a period of time.

Educational Quality and Assessment in Foreign Language

Several terms are used to refer to gathering information on foreign language learners, interpreting it, and making informed decisions in a systematic fashion. Although used interchangeably at times, the terms "testing," "assessment," and "evaluation" are not synonymous. Testing can be defined as a means of determining knowledge, and it refers to the performance of the task, written or oral. On the other hand, "assessment," according to Fenton (1996), "is the collection of relevant information that may be relied on for making decisions." When a standard and a decision-making system are applied "to assessment data to produce judgments about the amount and adequacy of the learning that has taken place," an evaluation is being made. The individuals making an informed decision are referred to as the "audience." The types of decisions that can be made are as varied as the types of possible audiences. In the schools, they are the teachers and learners, parents, board members, and administrators. Outside the schools, they may be legislators, policy makers, college admissions personnel, scholarship committees, and accreditation or funding agencies that are looking for feedback to assess the amount of learning that has taken place and the efficiency of the instruction.

Traditional assessment focuses on grades and ranking based on knowledge, curriculum, and skills. Classroom traditional assessment is based on quizzes, homework assignments, and standardized tests measuring the students' results against a norm (standardized norm-referenced tests) or a criterion (proficiency-based, criterion-referenced tests). The common practice of using standardized testing to measure students' aptitudes, knowledge, and skills has met with wide support because of several factors. Standardized tests can be administered easily at a relatively low cost, and since their results are quantitative, they can easily be analyzed through statistical procedures and reported or transmitted at a low cost, briefly and rapidly. As a consequence, the information they provide can be made available on a wide scale, allowing comparisons of student performance across school districts, states, and even international borders. Most policy-makers, government agencies, businesses, or media, appreciating the advantages these tests offer and the authority generally imparted to their numerical results, accept them as valid and reliable indicators of quality education. Meanwhile, they can easily overlook the considerable variations that may exist in standardized testing.

Standardized tests have several limitations, and questions are raised concerning their ability to measure accurately the quality of students' learning and performance, thereby revealing their inadequacy as a measure of what students know and can do (content standards). Both research and practice have suggested that teaching and testing should be closely connected. Oller pointed out that "perhaps the essential insight of a quarter of a century of language testing (both research and practice) is that good teaching and good testing are, or ought to be, nearly indistinguishable" (1991, p. 38). More recently, Terry stressed that "any material or technique that is effective for teaching a foreign language can also be used for testing" (1998, p. 277). As a consequence, when teachers and students aim toward foreign language content-standards-driven goals, striving to work with authentic materials and contexts and completing real-world tasks, a new paradigm for assessment is needed, calling for ongoing performance assessments of students' progress toward meeting these standards over a period of time.

Advances in research and theory and in technology indicate that it may be possible to better assess the quality of education and students' achievements by taking into account multiple indicators of a student's work. "Alternative assessment approaches," which focus on student-generated responses as opposed to choosing among proposed responses, as in standardized multiple-choice tests, are also designated as "authentic assessment," "performance-based assessment," and, more recently, "portfolio assessment."

Alternative Assessment and Portfolios

Authentic or performance-based assessment focuses on immediately observable results, implemented through standards, tasks, criteria, and scoring rubrics. Portfolio assessment adds another dimension, documenting the growth and development of students *over a period of time*. Through the process of selecting among their works and analyzing the selected works, students are led to self-evaluation and the setting of future goals.

Out of discussions at a conference on "Aggregating Portfolio Data" held by the Northwest Evaluation Association in Union, Washington, a group of educators from seven states, including F. Leon Paulson, Pearl R. Paulson and Carol A. Meyer, helped define a student's portfolio as "a purposeful collection of student work that exhibits the student's efforts, progress, and achievements. The collection must include student participation in selecting contents, the criteria for selection, the criteria for judging merit, and evidence of student self-reflection" (Paulson, Paulson, & Meyer, 1991, p. 60). Stiggins (1994) adds that a portfolio is also "a means of communicating about a student's growth and development," and is "not a form of assessment" per se (p. 87). However, it can be used very effectively for performance-based assessment because a portfolio holds examples of a student's work (artifacts), since some of those artifacts may be the results of performance assessment and because the reflection on that work transforms those artifacts into "evidence" of achievement.

One obvious advantage of portfolios is that they provide a richer picture of student performance than do more traditional, so-called "objective" forms of testing, and, most importantly, because they do so over a period of time. Traditional portfolios can be standards-based and may consist of ring binders, notebooks, or files divided into sections to organize the students' work and to document their level of achievement for each standard. These files and binders may be collected in drawers, boxes, or other large containers. Photographs, audiotapes, and videotapes have often been used to keep a record of students' work. Advances in technology have prompted the development of electronic and digital portfolios, which move both the process and the resulting product into another dimension.

The development of electronic and digital portfolios is supported by two main theoretical frameworks. Portfolio development literature (Danielson & Abrutyn, 1997) discusses collection, selection, reflection, and projection or direction. Multimedia development research (Ivers & Barron, 1998) is concerned with assessment and decision, design, development, implementation, and evaluation. Electronic and digital portfolios involve the use of electronic technologies to enable students and teachers to collect and organize artifacts in various media types (texts, graphs, audio, video, etc.) and establish hypertext links to organize that material and connect it across artifacts as well as to appropriate standards, especially in the case of the standards-based portfolios.

There is a difference between electronic and digital portfolios. Electronic portfolios contain artifacts that may be analyzed in analog form (e.g., videotapes), or may be in computer-readable form (e.g., word processor documents). Digital portfolios contain artifacts that have all been converted to computer-readable forms (e.g., digitized or scanned). I shall refer to them below simply as "electronic portfolios," leaving the degree of digital integration up to individual choices in planning, design, and implementation.

Students' electronic portfolios offer many advantages (Kankaanrana, Barrett, & Hartnell-Young, 2000; Kilbane & Milman, 2003), because of the process involved in creating them and because of the resulting products. The electronic portfolio is learner-centered, and its creation provides ample opportunities for incidental learning and can increase technological and multimedia skills and knowledge, from setting up folders to burning compact disks. It is an effective tool to demonstrate students' achievements and evidence of their having met standards, especially when it includes hypertext links to foreign language content standards and educational technology standards (at national, regional, or district levels). From a practical viewpoint, as opposed to traditional "files and boxes" portfolios, electronic portfolios use minimal storage space, are more portable, have a long shelf-life and make it easy to create backup files. They are also more easily and widely accessible and distributed, especially in the case of "Webfolios" (Nellen, 2000; Sheingold, 1992). If they are on the Web, they also enable the replaying of performance works at any time, and anywhere. On a more personal level, they can provide students and teachers with a sense of accomplishment, satisfaction, increased self esteem, and confidence, not only in their academic achievements but also in their ability to use technology. In both cases, students can perceive tangible evidence of their personal growth. Moreover, foreign language content standards and educational technology standards offer an ideal framework for planning and organizing an electronic portfolio, and most states have adopted them by now.

On the other hand, some major issues have been raised about electronic portfolios, including concerns about the infrastructure, the curriculum, the importance of reflection, high-stakes portfolios, and the audience. The infrastructure available in each school or classroom must be carefully considered: What types of technology are available to students? Does the school or classroom environment include computer equipment and software, network access, storage, publishing environment? How easy and frequent is their access? Questions concerning the curriculum include these: When and at what point in the curriculum is the concept of electronic portfolios introduced to the students? Does the curriculum include "appropriate" digital artifacts for electronic portfolios? Is a course planned in the curriculum for students to develop an electronic portfolio or at least get it underway? Does the curriculum include procedures to assess electronic portfolios?

Reflection is an important component of the portfolio process, since it is the step that moves portfolio development from mere gathering of data into a formative assessment and the learning process. At the 2000 American Educational Research Association conference, Breault raised questions about high-stakes portfolios and whether they include reflection, pointing out that they may undermine the formative aspect of reflective portfolios. In addition, Breault cautioned against the possible conflicting purposes, goals, and values between teacher and student in the development of high-stakes portfolios. Posting a portfolio on the Internet raises some specific audience issues regarding the quality and depth of reflection, intellectual property rights, security, and access.

Electronic portfolios and especially digital portfolios present some challenges in relation to the knowledge and skill levels they require with respect to the use of various types of hardware and software. They also require professional and technical support, expensive equipment, and a greater investment of time and energy, the flip side of often inspiring greater content, creativity, and depth. Furthermore, because not all members of the intended audience may have equal skills and access to electronic portfolios, the portfolios will be restricted to those with the skills and resources to view them.

Planning and Development of Foreign Language Student Portfolios

When planning a portfolio, one must always consider the purpose and the audience, both of which will determine many of the following context factors. Different audiences, students of varied ages and at different levels, will have distinct purposes and will require specific portfolio formats for storage, showcasing, assessment, presentation, and publication.

In *The Portfolio Connection*, Burke, Fogarty, and Belgrad (1994) propose several steps toward portfolio development. They include the following: *project* purposes, formulating the overall goals for the portfolio; *collect* and organize artifacts; *select* key artifacts, establishing priorities and determining what the content of the portfolio will include; *interject* personal style in the choices of design, cover, and layouts; *reflect*, labeling each artifact according to its meaning and value, explain why each artifact was selected and what its inclusion in the portfolio means; *inspect* to self-assess, indicating whether long-term and short-term goals are met and how, pointing out evidences of strengths and weaknesses; *perfect* and evaluate, refining the content and getting ready for evaluation or grading, bringing the portfolio to the stage of a polished final draft or a final product; *connect*, sharing the portfolio with someone, using it to establish a meaningful dialogue; *inject/eject* to refine and update the portfolio; and *respect* what has been accomplished by showing the portfolio to an audience.

From these 10 steps, the authors define three options for portfolio development: The *essential portfolio*, the most basic, involves three steps only: collect, select, and reflect. For the *expanded portfolio*, they add three steps and suggest these six: to project, collect, select, reflect, perfect, and connect. When all 10 steps are followed, the result is the *elaborated portfolio*. Burke, Fogarty, and Belgrad do not, however, include technology in the development of these portfolios.

In her analysis of portfolio development, Barrett (1999) uses Burke, Fogarty, and Belgrad's (1994) steps, but she includes technology and organizes the steps differently, giving some of them (e.g., connect) a slightly different meaning. She defines five stages of development and distinguishes different types of electronic portfolios. The first step remains defining portfolio contexts and goals, to be followed by the working portfolio, the reflective portfolio, the connected portfolio, and the presentation portfolio. They are supported by five levels of electronic sophistication based on "ease of use," including (1) word processing, (2) PowerPoint, database files or hypermedia stacks, (3) Adobe Acrobat plus audio and video files, (4) HTML-Web pages, and (5) multimedia authoring.

Two possible approaches are available in electronic portfolio development, whether one chooses to use generic tools or a customized system. The generic tools approach uses off-the-shelf software and more closely works on the model of collections of artifacts in file boxes or binders. Although the structure of the portfolio is then imposed by the developer of the chosen software, there is room for flexibility and creativity. If the cost for the infrastructure is lower, on the other hand, the cost for training is higher; however, once the procedure has started, students can continue to develop their portfolios, even after leaving the system.

The most common generic tools used to develop portfolios include relational databases (e.g., FileMaker Pro, Microsoft Access), hypermedia cards formats (e.g., HyperStudio, HyperCard, Digital Chisel, SuperLink and commercial templates), multimedia authoring software (e.g., Macromedia Authorware, Macromedia Director), network compatible hypermedia (e.g., HTML/WWW Pages, Adobe Acrobat/PDF), and office suite multimedia slide shows (e.g., PowerPoint, AppleWorks) (Barrett, 2001a, 2001b).

The customized approach requires designing a networked system or buying a proprietary software package. Although it offers record-keeping systems to collect artifacts and reflections, because it is highly structured and uses on-line databases, it can limit flexibility and creativity. The cost for infrastructure is high, but the cost for training may be lower, depending on the design of the system. A serious issue is what happens to the portfolios once students leave the system. In fact, there is no "best" electronic program to develop electronic portfolios. Choices depend on the assessment context, human and technological factors, such as students' technological skills, availability of personnel for professional and technical support, classroom and school equipment and schedules, and even school district infrastructure.

Foreign Language Student Electronic Portfolio Procedures

For all portfolios, the first step is to identify their purpose and primary audience. In the foreign language class, the content standards (what students should know and be able to do) will provide the goals and organizing framework, with the sample progress indicators defining the students' progress in meeting those standards. Identifying the foreign language content standards to be used is an essential component of student portfolio planning. Once identified, electronic folders can be set up to organize artifacts that will reflect the 5 *Cs* (Communication, Cultures,

Connections, Comparisons, and Communities) of the ACTFL Foreign Language Standards (National Standards in Foreign Language Education Project, 1996), as well as any existing state and local standards. When students plan electronic portfolios, they must consider national (and available state and local) educational technology standards, which are available at the International Society for Technology Education (ISTE) Web site, <http://www.iste.org/standards> and which should be part of the organizing framework. During this first stage, it will be necessary to identify all resources carefully: human resources (availability of personnel for professional and technical support and advice) and material support (hardware, software, time and curriculum constraints, skills constraints, and infrastructure).

In the second stage, collecting will be the primary activity of the students. The purposes, audiences, goals, and future use of these artifacts will determine their content. (Danielson & Abrutyn, 1997). Squirreling, packing, and storing will be the main skills required at that stage. The development of an electronic portfolio, an ongoing process that unfolds over a period of time, requires early planning, setting up an electronic filing system, and using high-density storing devices such as Zipdisks, Jaz disks, CD-ROM, and DVD-RAM.

Barton and Collins (1997) have suggested several types of evidence that can be collected for a portfolio. They include artifacts and documents produced through regular academic work, reproductions of student work produced outside the classroom, attestations documenting students' academic progress, and productions consisting of documents prepared specifically for the portfolios. These productions may be goal statements, students' personal interpretations of each specific purpose for their own portfolios, reflective statements written by students as they review and organize the evidence they have collected in their portfolios, and captions, that is, statements attached to each piece of evidence, articulating what it is, why it qualifies as evidence, and for what it stands as evidence (Barton & Collins). It is at the latter stage that students can interject their personal preferences by selecting appropriate multimedia to add their own style and individuality into their respective portfolios.

Stage three requires that students select the artifacts that best represent achievement of the standards and goals, write a general reflective statement on achieving each standard, and include specific reflective statements for each artifact chosen. They must elaborate on why each was selected and on its meaning and value for the portfolio. At this stage, Campbell, Melenyzer, Nettles, and Wyman (2000) and Campbell, Cignetti, Melenyzer, Nettles, and Wyman (2001) suggest three helpful questions: "What?" "So what?" "Now what?" They explain:

> To use these questions, the student would first summarize the artifact that documents the experience, in order to answer the question "What?" Second, the student would reflect on what he or she learned and how this leads to meet the standard, which answers the question "So what?" And third, the student would address implications for future learning needed and set forth refinements or adaptations, in order to answer "Now what?" (Campbell, Melenyzer, et al., p. 22)

Such questions can easily be used as reflective prompts, and the last one will lead students to notice patterns in the work they have collected, and to "project," that is, to look ahead and set goals for future learning (Danielson & Abrutyn, 1997). Through this reflection and analysis, students become increasingly aware of themselves as learners. This awareness is the major step that separates a good portfolio from a multimedia presentation, a glorified electronic résumé, or a digital scrapbook and moves portfolio development from mere gathering of data into formative assessment and learning process, turning it into a powerful developmental tool. Students will also need to select appropriate technology tools and strategies in order to enhance style, to individualize their portfolios, and to digitize images, audio recordings, and video artifacts.

In the next stage, students organize the digital artifacts and establish connections, creating hypermedia links among standards, artifacts, and reflections. Through the linking process they will identify patterns, then review and edit their portfolios and goals, and share their portfolios to gain feedback and make necessary improvements. In this case, linking becomes learning. The transformation of artifacts into evidence is not always clear. Linking reflections, artifacts and standards makes the thinking process more explicit. Moreover, creating links from multiple perspectives and goals overcomes the linearity of the two-dimensional portfolio (Barrett, 1998). This process should lead students to making decisions on future learning based on their portfolios.

The fifth and final stage leads to the presentation of the portfolio, real or virtual, before the selected audience. But it must first be recorded (i.e., published) to an appropriate presentation and storage medium (WWW, CDs, video, DVD).

An Ongoing Process Over Time

The development of an electronic portfolio is clearly not one linear process, but rather a sequence that follows an iterative path, developing over time as well as representing the students' work over a period of time. Collecting and selecting artifacts should be an ongoing endeavor, whereby students are encouraged to become "digital pack rats" (Barrett, 1998). Planning for an electronic portfolio from the start is a sound choice, as it will help set up an electronic filing system at an early date. It will also encourage students not to leave either the collection or the selection to the last minute. Another helpful early step is to identify the foreign language content standards and the educational technology standards to be used as an organizing framework. Electronic folders are created to store artifacts for each standard, cross referencing those that demonstrate evidence of achieving and meeting more than one standard. On an ongoing basis, sound clips and video clips should be digitized and edited, using editing software (e.g., Sound Companion, Kaboom!, Movie Player Pro, Avid Cinema, Adobe Premiere, or Final Cut).

The organization of the portfolio should be an ongoing process that includes the creation of hypertext links among standards, artifacts, and reflections as the connections are identified; and the insertion of bookmarks, thumbnails, movie links, sound clips, and "buttons." A portfolio matrix, using a spreadsheet or a simple word processor table, can provide a single-page overview of such artifacts and their connections. Through the use of a database program or a PDF form with fields, a standard form can be designed to record reflective comments on each artifact and each standard. Barrett (1998) also recommends the creation of an outline or story board, using word processor with outlining (e.g., Microsoft Word), slide show with outlining (e.g., PowerPoint), or mapping software (e.g., Inspiration). Because a table of contents is not only helpful, but necessary, as is keeping it current, Barrett (2001a) proposes using a table to provide such information as a "Portfolio at a Glance."

The construction of an electronic portfolio should at first be considered a year-long project, yet one should keep in mind that it can be developed to cover a longer period of time and can be carried out throughout a student career.

References

Barrett, H. C. (1998). Feature article: Strategic questions: What to consider when planning for electronic portfolios, *Learning & Leading with Technology 25*(2): 6-13.

Barrett, H. C. (1999). *Electronic teaching portfolios.* Paper presented at the Society for Information Technology and Teacher Education (SITE) Annual Conference, San Antonio. Retrieved January 4, 2004, from http://electronicportfolios.com/portfolios/site2000.html

Barrett, H. C. (2001a). *ICT Support for electronic portfolios and alternative assessment: State of the art.* Retrieved January 4, 2004, from http://www.electronicportfolios.com/portfolios/wcce2001.pdf

Barrett, H. C. (2001b). Electronic portfolios = Multimedia development + portfolio development: The electronic portfolio development process. In B. L. Cambridge (Ed.), *Electronic portfolios: Emerging practices for students, faculty, and institutions* (pp. 110-111). American Association for Higher Education. Retrieved January 4, 2004, from http://www.electronicportfolios.com/portfolios/EPDevProcess.html

Barton, J., & Collins, A., Eds. (1997). *Portfolio assessment: A handbook for educators.* Menlo Park, CA: Addison Wesley.

Breault, R. A. (2000, April). *Metacognition in portfolio development.* Paper presented in session titled "Reflective Writing and Portfolios: What is the Quality of Preservice Teachers' Thinking?" at the meeting of the American Educational Research Association, New Orleans, LA.

Burke, K., Fogarty, R., & Belgrad, S. (1994). *The mindful school: The portfolio connection.* Arlington Heights, IL: Skylight Training & Publishing.

Campbell, D. M., Melenyzer, B. J., Nettles, D. H., & Wyman, R. M. (2000). *Portfolio and performance assessment in teacher education.* Boston: Allyn & Bacon.

Campbell, D. M., Cignetti, P. M., Melenyzer, B. J., Nettles, D. H., & Wyman, R. M. (2001). *How to develop a professional portfolio: A manual for teachers* (2nd ed.). Boston: Allyn & Bacon.

Danielson, C., & Abrutyn, L. (1997). *An introduction to using portfolios in the classroom.* Alexandria, VA: Association for Supervision and Curriculum Development (ASCD).

Fenton, R. (1996). Performance assessment system development. *Alaska Educational Research Journal, 2*(1): 13-22.

Ivers, K., & Barron, A. E. (1998). *Multimedia projects in education.* Englewood, CO: Libraries Unlimited.

Kankaanrana, M., Barrett, H. C., & Hartnell-Young, E. (2001). Exploring the use of electronic portfolios in international contexts. *Proceedings of World Conference on Educational Media, Hypermedia, and Telecommunications (Ed-Media) 2001*(1): 874-876. Retrieved January 4, 2004, http://dl.aace.org/8614

Kilbane, C. R., & Milman, N. B. (2003). *What every teacher should know about creating digital teaching portfolios.* Boston: Allyn & Bacon.

National Standards in Foreign Language Education Project (1996). *Standards for foreign language learning: Preparing for the 21st century.* Yonkers, NY: ACTFL.

Nellen, T. (1999). Using the web for high school student-writers. In S. Gruber (Ed.), *Weaving a virtual web: Practical approaches to new information technologies* (pp. 219-225). Urbana, IL: National Council of Teachers of English. Retrieved January 4, 2004, from http://www.tnellen.com/ted/weave.html

Oller, J. (1991). Foreign language testing: Its breadth. *ADFL Bulletin, 22*(3): 33-38.

Paulson, F. L., Paulson, P. R., & Meyer, C. A. (1991). What makes a portfolio a portfolio? *Educational Leadership 48*(5): 60-63.

Sheingold, K. (1992, June). *Technology and assessment.* Paper presented at the Technology & School Reform Conference, Dallas, TX.

Stiggins, R. J. (1994). *Student-centered classroom assessment.* New York: Merrill.

Terry, R. M. (1998). Authentic tasks and materials for testing in the foreign language classroom. In J. Harper, M. G. Lively, & M. K. Williams (Eds.), *The coming of age of the profession: Issues and emerging ideas for the teaching of foreign languages* (pp. 277-290). Boston: Heinle & Heinle.

4

Assessing Readiness of Foreign Language Education Majors to Take the Praxis II Exam

Carol Wilkerson
Carson-Newman College

Judith H. Schomber
Georgia Southern University

Jana Sandarg
Augusta State University

Abstract

Ten of the 13 states in the Southern Conference on Language Teaching (SCOLT) region require the Praxis II Exam for teacher licensure in French, German, or Spanish. Perceptions of high failure rates on this exam call into question the quality of teacher education programs. Test takers and reviewers find required tasks and performance levels on the Praxis II unaligned with the expectations for beginning teachers established by the American Council on the Teaching of Foreign Languages (ACTFL). After describing the sections of the exam and their limitations, this article offers strategies to prepare students for the tasks required and ways to assess student readiness to take the exam.

Background

Most states within the SCOLT region have adopted the Praxis II Exams as licensure instruments for prospective teachers of French, German, and Spanish. For state departments of education, the Praxis II Series has become an attractive and practical alternative to state-generated licensure exams because Educational Testing Service (ETS), a professional test development company based in Princeton, New Jersey, assumes responsibility for test development and administration, along with liability for legal issues. An additional benefit to states and teachers is licensure reciprocity among states requiring the Praxis II Exams. Unfortunately, however, the media report that prospective foreign language teachers, especially in the field of Spanish, fail the exam in alarming numbers and must often repeat the exam multiple times (Cumming, 1998). Test takers and teacher educators respond that the expectations of the component tests surpass reasonable levels of professional knowledge and skill for beginning teachers.

The Higher Education Amendments of 1998 require institutions to publish a "report card" that includes pass rates on teacher certification tests and a comparison of the institutional pass rate with state averages (National Research Council, 2000). This report can be particularly damaging to foreign language education programs because they tend to have smaller numbers of majors and because failure rates often include the scores of test takers who are not students or graduates of an institution (Educational Testing Service, 1998). Reports may be further skewed if institutions have low numbers of test takers. The *ETS Background Report* (1998) shows that 90% of the reporting institutions had 10 or fewer students taking a particular Praxis II Test. With numbers this low, a single failure has the potential to endanger a teacher education program. Furthermore, failure rates are high because students often take the licensure test as practice, even though they know that they are not prepared. Sudzina (2001) states that Praxis II Tests are usually taken between the junior and senior years of college, too early to assess whether students know the specialty content.

This article begins with a comparison of state policies regarding the Praxis II in the SCOLT region. It continues with an overview of two of the component tests of the Praxis II and an assessment of their limitations. The discussion concludes with strategies to prepare test takers for the Praxis II and ways to assess candidate readiness to take the licensure exam.

Comparing State Options and Policies

State officials choose the component tests in the Praxis Series for use as licensure instruments in their respective states, and they also establish the passing scores. Teachers and university faculty may be asked for input, but they do not set policy (Nweke & Hall, 1999). During the adoption process in Georgia, for example, the Professional Standards Commission (PSC) invited panels of teachers and teacher educators to critique two Praxis tests and to suggest passing scores. However, the PSC ultimately selected the component tests currently in use and established the initial ("phase-in") passing scores for the various Praxis II Exams.

The summative data displayed in Table 1 reveal five permutations of the Praxis Exam currently in use in the SCOLT region: (1) the German language tes, (2) the Content Knowledge Test only, (3) the Productive Language Skills Test only, (4) a combination of the Content Knowledge Test and Productive Language Skills Tests, and (5) a combination of the Content Knowledge Test and three tests of Principles of Learning and Teaching for grades K-12. Therefore, comparisons of Praxis scores and requirements by states cannot be made without an *a priori* explanation of terms and specification of which tests are in use. Table 1 compares the various state options in the SCOLT region.

Table 1
Comparison of Component Tests and Passing Scores
by States in SCOLT Region

State	French Tests and Passing Scores	German Tests and Passing Scores	Spanish Tests and Passing Scores
Arkansas	Content Knowledge 158 Productive Skills 167		Content Knowledge 155 Productive Skills 141
Georgia	Content Knowledge 156 Productive Skills 169	Content Knowledge 156 Productive Skills 182	Content Knowledge 167 Productive Skills 159
Kentucky	Content Knowledge 159 Principles of Learning & Teaching (PLT) PLT Grades K-6 161 PLT Grades 5-9 161 PLT Grades 7-12 161	Content Knowledge 157 Principles of Learning & Teaching (PLT) PLT Grades K-6 161 PLT Grades 5-9 161 PLT Grades 7-12 161	Content Knowledge 160 Principles of Learning & Teaching (PLT) PLT Grades K-6 161 PLT Grades 5-9 161 PLT Grades 7-12 161
Louisiana	Content Knowledge 156	German Test 500	Content Knowledge 160
Mississippi	Productive Skills 161	Productive Skills 160	Productive Skills 155
North Carolina	Content Knowledge and Productive Skills combined score of 335, no minimum on either test	Content Knowledge 153	Content Knowledge and Productive Skills combined score of 327, no minimum on either test
South Carolina	Content Knowledge 156 Productive Skills 166	Content Knowledge 151 Productive Skills 181	Content Knowledge 148 Productive Skills 161
Tennessee	Content Knowledge 160 Productive Skills 165	Content Knowledge 139	Content Knowledge 152 Productive Skills 154
Virginia	Content Knowledge 169	Content Knowledge 162	Content Knowledge 161
West Virginia	Content Knowledge 131	Content Knowledge 132	Content Knowledge 143

Information retrieved and compiled from <www.ets.org/praxis/prxstate.html> November 1, 2003 (Educational Testing Service, 2003b).

Although states show near consensus in their required passing score for the French Productive Language Skills Test (number 0171), with only eight points separating the highest and lowest minimum passing scores, minimum passing scores for the French Content Knowledge Test (number 0173) differ by 38 points. The states that require the Productive Language Skills Test in German (number 0182) differ by 22 points in their minimum passing scores, and scores for the German Content Knowledge (number 0181) test vary by 30 points. The minimum passing scores for the Productive Language Skills Test in Spanish (number 0192) vary by 20 points and the difference grows to 24 points for scores on the Spanish Content Knowledge Test (number 0191). The combined minimum passing scores for the French and Spanish Praxis tests in North Carolina exceed those of every state in the region requiring the same tests. These multiple state options regarding test choice and the range of state policies regarding passing scores on the Praxis make comparing data difficult. Moreover, teachers seeking licensure in the same language in the same region of the country are, in reality, held to different expectations depending upon the policy adopted by the state in which they seek licensure. The National Research Council (2000) reached this same conclusion in its comparison of state licensure exams. These differences beg questions of fairness and realistic expectations for beginning K-12 language teachers.

It should be noted that states were encouraged to adopt the Praxis II Exams to facilitate certification reciprocity by using a common licensure instrument. However, the National Association of State Directors of Teacher Education and Certification (NASDTEC) Interstate Contract agreements essentially guarantee transferability of teaching certificates with little regard for Praxis scores, as illustrated in Table 2. Table 2 also shows that the 10 states in the SCOLT region requiring the Praxis II Exams have reciprocity agreements with Alabama, Florida, and Texas—the three states that do not require the Praxis II.

Table 2
Licensure Reciprocity in the SCOLT Region

State	NASDTEC Interstate Contract	Additional Requirements Beyond Valid Certificate from Other State
Alabama	With all SCOLT states	3 years' experience in last 7 years
Arkansas	With all SCOLT states	
Florida	With all SCOLT states	
Georgia	With all SCOLT states	
Kentucky	With all SCOLT states except MS & LA	2 years' experience in field
Louisiana	With all SCOLT states except KY	Must meet LA's Praxis II scores
Mississippi	With all SCOLT states except KY	2 years' experience in field
North Carolina	With all SCOLT states	Must meet NC's Praxis II scores
South Carolina	With all SCOLT states	27 months of teaching experience in field
Tennessee	With all SCOLT states	Exemption from Praxis II reviewed case-by-case
Texas	With all SCOLT states	Test scores from Praxis II reviewed case-by-case
Virginia	With all SCOLT states	
West Virginia	With all SCOLT states	Exemption from Praxis II reviewed case-by-case

Information retrieved and compiled November 1, 2003, from the Web site of the National Association of State Directors of Teacher Education and Certification: <www.nasdtec.org>.

The Content Knowledge and Productive Language Skills Tests

Within the SCOLT region the most frequently used component tests in the Praxis Series are the Content Knowledge Test (number 0173 in French, 0181 in German, and 0191 in Spanish) and the Productive Language Skills Test (number 0171 in French, 0182 in German, and 0192 in Spanish). Louisiana is the only state to use German test number 0180. As of September 1, 2003, Kentucky requires teachers to pass three Principles of Learning and Teaching Tests (PLT) for grades K-6, grades 5-9, and grades 7-12, in addition to the Content Knowledge Test for each language.

The *Tests at a Glance* (*TAAG*) booklet (Educational Testing Service, 2003b) states that the Content Knowledge Test in each language (French, German, and Spanish) assesses the knowledge and competencies necessary for a beginning or entry-year teacher of the target language. Each 2-hour test of 120 multiple-choice questions includes tape-recorded listening passages and printed material, with questions on various language skills and cultural knowledge. The first section tests interpretative listening, requiring test takers to answer within a 30-minute period 32 questions based upon an unspecified number of aural recordings of native speakers talking at a normal rate of conversation. Questions assess "phonemic discrimination, understanding of idiomatic expressions, familiarity with vocabulary and typical conversational structures, and comprehension of important facts or ideas contained in the spoken material."

The second section of the Content Knowledge Test lasts 35 minutes and contains 34 questions that assess knowledge of the structure of the target language. Test takers analyze spoken (recorded) and written errors in the respective target language. Depending upon the language tested, questions focus on "grammar, mechanics, morphology, phonology, syntax, word analysis, unacceptable Anglicisms, use of slang, vocabulary, and word choice."

In the third section, interpretative reading, test takers have 35 minutes to answer 31 questions based upon an unspecified number of reading selections. The *TAAG* describes the passages as encompassing a variety of topics at various levels of difficulty, from print and nonprint sources, such as periodicals, the Internet, advertisements, and literature.

The fourth section tests knowledge of cultural perspectives. Test takers have 20 minutes to answer 23 questions about "geography, history, lifestyles and societies, literature and fine arts, and sociolinguistic elements" of French, German, or Spanish. On the French test, questions are written in English and French; on the German and Spanish tests, questions are asked in the target language.

The *TAAG* describes the Productive Language Skills test as a one-hour test with two sections–speaking, worth 60% of the final score, and writing, worth 40%. There are six spoken questions to be answered in the 25 minutes allotted. The skills tested in the speaking section include "role-playing, picture description, giving instructions or picture narration, stating and defending an opinion, oral paraphrase of a listening passage, and making a brief talk." The *TAAG* offers test takers one sample question for this portion of the test. In the writing section, test takers have

35 minutes "to write a short composition based on a series of pictures, to write a short formal letter, and to write four questions to elicit short and long answers." However, the *TAAG* offers no sample questions for this section.

Limitations of the Praxis II Exam

A closer look at the Content Knowledge and Productive Skills Tests reveals problems with test questions and instructions. During workshops and professional conferences (Bernardy, Leger, Sandarg, & Wilkerson, 2003; Sandarg, Schomber, & Wilkerson, 1999a; 1999b; Sandarg & Wilkerson, 2002; Sandarg, Wilkerson, & Riley, 2002), test takers and educators reported that the tasks on the Content Knowledge Test differ significantly from activities in contemporary foreign language classrooms. Test takers state that dialogues and narrations are read only once and are frequently followed by multiple questions. Instructions in the listening section do not indicate whether test takers should listen for global meaning or discrete items of information; therefore, test takers try to retain all the information, thereby taxing their normal memory load. Whereas typical classroom listening tasks occur in a context that provides a degree of predictability or a frame of reference for the listener, directions to test takers in the *TAAG* state only that they will hear short conversations or narrations. In the Structure of the Language section of the Content Knowledge Test, students are asked to find student errors in aural and written sentences, a task inconsistent with current teaching practices, which encourage students to speak, errors and all, as they develop proficiency.

Although the reading portion of the Content Knowledge Test purports to evaluate students' abilities to generalize, deduce, or infer, the types and lengths of reading passages lead students to believe that they have been tested on literary knowledge rather than on reading skills. Test takers advise other students to memorize facts about authors, genres, and literary works prior to taking the Praxis II. Furthermore, specialized vocabulary and low-frequency idioms limit students' ability to make inferences or educated guesses. And junior-level students who take the Praxis II are often just developing the skills to understand abstract ideas as they read in the foreign language.

The *TAAG* description of the Cultural Perspectives portion of the Content Knowledge Test covers a wide range of topics, including history, geography, literature and the arts, life-styles, and sociolinguistic elements in French-, German-, and Spanish-speaking countries and regions. Preparing for this portion of the test is, therefore, a formidable task. It is particularly daunting for Spanish students, since Spanish is spoken in 20 countries, as well as in the United States. No typical foreign language major can be expected to assimilate the breadth of knowledge required to prepare for the culture test, and the ensuing process is tantamount to a game of Trivial Pursuit™, a concern also noted by Mitchell and Barth (1999) in Praxis Tests of other disciplines.

The tasks required of students in the speaking and writing sections of the Productive Skills Test are aligned with those practiced in today's classroom. Students are familiar with picture description, role-playing, giving instructions, picture nar-

rations, and writing compositions and letters. However, the proficiency requirements of many of the tasks surpass what is reasonably expected of entry-level teachers, according to ACTFL recommendations. For example, students are asked to
defend an opinion, a task at the Superior Level of the ACTFL proficiency scale.
The recommended proficiency level for a beginning teacher is Advanced Low, a
level at which test takers should be able "to narrate and describe in all major time
frames in paragraph-length discourse" (Breiner-Sanders, Lowe, Miles, & Swender,
2000). Undergraduates typically take the Praxis II at the end of their junior year or
in the beginning of their senior year, prior to student teaching. With only 2 or 3
years of college experience in the language, few students will have achieved Advanced-Low proficiency, much less the Superior Level.

Obstacles to test takers are not confined to the test instrument itself; poor testing conditions hamper even the best students. Test takers have told the authors of
problems ranging from unbearable room temperatures and no bathroom breaks to
faulty equipment and conflicting directions from test monitors. Proctors have ar-
rived up to an hour late, and at other times they have given procedural instructions
contradicting those in the test booklet. When tests had to be rescheduled by ETS,
students learned of their retest dates only 48 hours in advance, causing them to
scramble to change schedules and secure release time from work or school. Perhaps most stressful and distracting is the practice of placing students side by side to
record on cassette tape recorders in an open room with background noise of different voices and languages. Such testing conditions annoy students and heighten
frustration and stress. These sorts of problems must be eliminated if students are to
be successful.

In 2002 the Educational Testing Service (ETS) began revising the Content
Knowledge and Productive Skills Tests with input from foreign language educators and classroom teachers. A comparison of the former and current descriptions
of the tests in the on-line *TAAG* reveals three changes. The current Content Knowledge Test contains 20 fewer questions; the listening and reading passages focus on
interpretative listening and *interpretive* reading; and ETS defines sympathetic and
unsympathetic readers and listeners in the scoring guide for the Productive Skills
Tests.

Preparing for the Praxis

Educational Testing Service sells 17 different study guides and kits and 18
distinct diagnostic preparation programs, described as covering material on the
test, with suggested test-taking strategies, actual full-length tests, a scoring key, an
explanation of answers, and an explanation of scoring procedures. In the *TAAG*
these are marketed as "A great way to study!" However, nothing is available for
French, German, or Spanish. This fact, coupled with the paucity of sample items in
the *Tests at a Glance*, leaves foreign language test takers very little with which to
practice for the Praxis II Exam. To help test takers prepare, many colleges of education suggest that their faculty take the Praxis II to get an idea about the types of
questions students are likely to encounter (Sudzina, 2001). Another way that teacher

educators might gather information about the component Praxis II tests is by studying the Praxis Series *Job Analysis* for the respective language to be tested (Reynolds, 1993; Tannenbaum, 1992; 1994).

These *Job Analyses* contain the original statements that guided the ETS teams as they revised the former National Teacher Examination to become the Praxis Series. The statements reveal the Praxis philosophy regarding what entry-level, newly licensed (certified) teachers should know and be able to do. Setting aside foreign language pedagogy, which is not included in the Content Knowledge and Productive Language Skills Tests, educators will note the similarity of the content areas to the traditional four skills of reading, writing, listening, and speaking, with a separate cultural component. The final area, structure of the language, closely resembles contrastive analysis, emphasizing error analysis of Anglo non-native speakers of the target language. To this end, teacher educators can help language education majors by familiarizing them with the tenets of error analysis and contrastive analysis and by providing sample texts from this long-gone era of the profession. Two such texts are *The Grammatical Structures of English and German: A Contrastive Sketch* (Kufner, 1962) and *The Grammatical Structures of English and Spanish* (Stockwell, Martin, & Bowen, 1965).

The wording of the original statements also cues teacher educators to the linguistic and grammatical terms with which students must be familiar to be successful on the exam. For example, statements in Appendix C of the Spanish *Job Analysis* (Tannenbaum, 1992) inform test takers that they must demonstrate the correct formation and use of regular and irregular verbs (including orthographic- and stem-changing) in all indicative tenses, in the conditional, and the subjunctive mood, as well as the passive voice and its reflexive or active-voice substitutes. Test takers must understand morphemes, augmentative, diminutive, and pejorative suffixes. They must also understand the formation of compound words and contractions, and the function of cognates and false cognates in the development of vocabulary. In addition, test takers must identify common pronunciation problems for nonnative speakers of Spanish, such as the trill and tap [r]. Knowledge of the language must be complemented with knowledge *about* the language as well as knowledge about *how Anglophones learn* the target language.

Teacher educators can help prepare test takers by pointing out to them the varying degrees of contextual cues in the reading passages for the three languages in the *TAAG*. For example, the French example provides background information that test takers use to interpret the passage. The text is followed by a single question. The German example is an advertisement, likely found in a newspaper or telephone book. German test takers use visual cues to answer a single question. However, the Spanish example, by contrast, is comprised of three paragraphs of written text without title, background information, or visual cues. Sentences average 20 words in length, and three sentences contain 28 or more words. Clearly, the amount of background information, the length, and the level of difficulty of reading passages vary.

To prepare language education majors for this range of texts, teacher educators might select reading passages of varying lengths and genres and remove normal contextual cues, such as titles, headings, and repetitions. Since contemporary best practice instructs students to rely upon schema and background knowledge, foreign language education majors may need overt instruction on how to make inferences when reading unfamiliar texts with minimal or no background information or normal discourse cues.

The final section of the Content Knowledge Test assesses beginning teachers' knowledge of the target culture. In order to prepare language education majors for the possible topics indicated in the *TAAG,* faculty should advise majors to complete at least one course, if not more, in literature, in culture, and in history prior to taking the Praxis II Exam. Language faculty can compile lists in their respective specialty areas for students to study for this portion of the test. Topics should include famous artists, writers, performers, Nobel Prize winners, geographical features of countries and regions where the target language is spoken, typical regional foods, and significant dates and events in history. Test-takers should take comfort, however, in knowing that even native speakers frequently say that they have not known the answers to all the questions in the culture section of the test.

The *General Tips* on preparing for the Praxis Productive Language Skills Tests, found in the supplemental *Advice on Taking the Productive Language Skills Tests* (Educational Testing Service, 2003a), may mislead test-takers by indicating that they have to demonstrate a thorough knowledge of basic verb tenses on this exam. No explanation is given for what is meant by the phrase *basic verb tenses*; therefore, teacher education faculty need to point out that expectations in the *Job Analyses* indicate that students need a thorough knowledge of *all* verb tenses. Students should be advised to complete advanced grammar course work before taking the Praxis Exam.

As stated earlier, the *TAAG* for the Productive Language Skills Test includes only one sample question for the speaking section and none for the writing section. The on-line *Advice on Taking the Productive Language Skills Tests* gives some ideas of ways to practice, such as opening a magazine to an interesting picture and explaining within a 2-minute time limit in the target language what has just happened, what is happening now, and what will probably happen next. However, the *TAAG* states that test takers are evaluated on their comprehensibility to *educated* native speakers, their ability to communicate *without major errors* in grammar and vocabulary, and their ability to *defend* an opinion (emphasis added). These abilities are hallmarks of Superior proficiency, as defined by ACTFL, surpassing its recommendation of Advanced-Low proficiency for beginning K-12 teachers. The scoring guide for both the writing and speaking sections awards the highest rating (a score of four) to responses that are *completely* and easily comprehensible, even to an *unsympathetic* listener/reader (defined by ETS as a native speaker not accustomed to dealing with nonnative learners), to responses that are *completely* and *entirely* accurate/relevant, and to responses that employ a *broad, precise* vocabulary adequate for *almost all topics* (emphasis added). Again, these are hallmarks of Superior proficiency. Perhaps the best strategy to prepare majors for this reality is for faculty to talk openly about the expectations of proficiency early in students' academic careers, even setting proficiency criteria for admission to teacher candidacy. Other strategies might include requiring oral interviews with prospective majors to assess proficiency, establishing expectations of written and oral proficiency in courses required of language majors, and maintaining portfolios of students' course work to assess proficiency rather than relying upon end-of-course grades when determining readiness to take the Praxis Exam. Candid discussion about and periodic assessment of students' proficiency should become the responsibility of all faculty, not only those who teach the foreign language education courses.

Best Practices for Beginning Teachers

It is essential for test takers to adequately prepare for the Praxis II by using the *TAAG* and the suggestions listed above. However, long before it is their time to take the Praxis II, foreign language education majors can be positioned for success by achieving the desired level of language proficiency. Since the proficiency level for success on the Praxis II is above Advanced Low, educators must take steps to ensure that foreign language majors reach high levels of proficiency before they take the test.

All foreign language majors should be encouraged to participate in a study-abroad program in which they will have structured classes to continue their formal study of the language and in which they will have enriched out-of-class experiences to enhance their language skills and their cultural competence. The study-abroad experience, as Riedel (1989), Milleret (1990), and Talburt and Stewart (1999) have pointed out, is still far too loosely structured and not well enough assessed to assure that the participant is moving toward Advanced Low proficiency by engaging in frequent informal conversations with native speakers and narrating and describing in present, past, and future tenses.

Pre-service teachers also can benefit from maintaining a portfolio of their language development as they prepare for the Praxis II. In the same way that students can build a reflective portfolio of classroom teaching and observations of students and situations, as Antonek, McCormick, and Donato (1997) suggest, students with the assistance of foreign language educators can compile a list of language tasks at the Advanced and Superior Levels and record the completion of such tasks, their frequency, and any comments on their performance. Tasks can be accomplished through normal classroom work, service-learning projects, or other means through which students interact with native speakers.

Foreign language professionals can facilitate the process of moving their students toward the Advanced and Superior Levels by supporting initiatives to begin foreign languages in elementary school as Oxford (1998) suggests. If beginning teachers are to attain high levels of proficiency, they must begin language study in elementary school to gain the necessary 720 hours at middle, high, and college levels (Malone, Rifkin, Christian, & Johnson, 2003). At the same time, progression in formal language programs must be well articulated to prevent students from repeating at the next higher level what they have already learned at a lower level, a circumstance that occurs frequently in U.S. colleges and universities. It is common to find students with considerable backgrounds in foreign language study from elementary, middle, and high school enrolled in elementary foreign language courses at the postsecondary level.

Many European countries design a national curriculum with a clear progression of learning to higher levels of proficiency in foreign languages. With the publication of the *Standards for Foreign Language Learning in the 21st Century* (ACTFL, 1999), educators in all states have a guide for both curriculum and articulation. Many states, such as Georgia, have aligned their state curriculum for foreign languages to the National Standards, including assessments of learning. Sandrock (1996) suggests that articulation is best achieved through a focus on the progression of student learning, rather than by grade levels or the implementation of curriculum guides based on strict sequences.

Finally, the standard undergraduate language curriculum must be reexamined to determine if higher-level proficiency elements are incorporated into classroom goals and activities. In upper-division courses in literature and civilization, for example, there must be a deliberate attempt to "push" students toward high levels of proficiency with speaking and writing activities designed to generate student performance at that level, rather than heavy reliance on lectures, listening, and note-taking. The National Council for Accreditation of Teacher Education (NCATE), in approving the *Program Standards for Foreign Language Teacher Education* (ACTFL, 2002), specifies content areas that are almost universally addressed in upper-division foreign language courses. Greater efforts must therefore be made to develop a collaborative relationship between departments of foreign languages and teacher education units within colleges and universities.

Assessing Readiness

As foreign language educators, we must do all we can to ensure that our students are ready to take the Praxis II Exam. We must teach and evaluate our students with communicative methods, encourage them to study abroad, and incorporate service-learning and community connections into our program curriculum. And although it is exceedingly difficult for students to develop proficiency at the Advanced or Superior Levels of the ACTFL scale after 2 to 3 years of college study, we must help them reach these levels. We must prepare students for the Praxis II Exam by reviewing, and perhaps overtly teaching, test-taking skills. Some educators suggest that we teach to the test. The strategies outlined in this article do not solve all the problems associated with the Praxis II in its current form, but they form a tool that foreign language educators can use to assess student readiness to take the Exam.

References

American Council on the Teaching of Foreign Languages (ACTFL). (2002). *Program standards for the preparation of foreign language teachers (Initial level—undergraduate and graduate: For K-12 and secondary certification programs).* Yonkers, NY: ACTFL. Retrieved January 7, 2004, from http://www.actfl.org/public/articles/ncate2002.pdf

Antonek, J., McCormick, D., & Donato, R. (1997). The student teacher portfolio as autobiography: Developing a professional identity. *The Modern Language Journal, 81,* 15-27.

Bernardy, A., Leger, T., Sandarg, J., & Wilkerson, C. (2003, February). *Success on the Praxis II Exam in French, German, and Spanish.* Paper and workshop presented at the annual meeting of The Southern Conference on Language Teaching, Atlanta, GA.

Breiner-Sanders, K., Lowe, P., Miles, J., & Swender, E. (2000). ACTFL proficiency guidelines–Speaking. *Foreign Language Annals, 33,* 13-18.

Cumming, Doug. (1998, December 20). One-fifth fail test to be teacher. *The Atlanta Journal-Constitution,* p. C1.

Educational Testing Service. (2003a). *Advice on taking the productive language skills test: Supplement to the languages tests at a glance.* Princeton, NJ. Retrieved January 7, 2004, from ftp://ftp.ets.org/pub/tandl/plstip.pdf

Educational Testing Service. (2003b). *Tests at a glance: Languages.* Princeton, NJ. Retrieved January 7, 2004, from http://www.ets.org/praxis/prxstate.html

Educational Testing Service. (1998). The use of Praxis pass rates to evaluate teacher educational programs. An ETS background report. (ERIC Document Reproduction Service No. ED 435 640)

Kufner, H. (1962). *The grammatical structures of English and German: A contrastive sketch.* Chicago: University of Chicago Press.

Malone, M., Rifkin, B., Christian, D., & Johnson, D. (2003). Attaining high levels of proficiency: Challenges for foreign language education in the United States. *ERIC/CLL News Bulletin, 26.*

Milleret, M. (1990). Evaluation and the summer language program abroad: A review essay. *The Modern Language Journal, 74,* 483-488.

Mitchell, R., & Barth, P. (1999). *Not good enough: A content analysis of teacher licensing examinations. How teacher licensing tests fall short.* Washington, DC: Educational Trust. (ERIC Document Reproduction Service No. ED 457 261)

National Association of State Directors of Teacher Education and Certification (NASDTEC). Web site: www.nasdtec.org

National Research Council. (2000). *Tests and teaching quality: Interim report.* Committee on Assessment and Teaching Quality, Board on Testing and Assessment. Washington, DC: National Academy Press.

National Standards in Foreign Language Education Project. (1999). *Standards for foreign language learning in the 21st century.* Yonkers, NY: Author.

Nweke, W., & Hall, T. (1999). *Evaluating cut-scores on two certification tests: How well do decisions based on cut-scores match teacher- and principal-reported ratings of competence in the classroom?* Paper presented at the annual meeting of the American Educational Research Association, Montreal, Quebec, Canada. (ERIC Document Reproduction Service No. ED 457 261)

Oxford, R. (1998). Where is the United States headed with K-12 foreign language education? *ERIC/CLL News Bulletin, 22.*

Reynolds, A. (1993). Knowledge and skills for the beginning German teacher. Princeton, NJ: Educational Testing Service. (ERIC Document Reproduction Service No. ED 382 653)

Riedel, K. (1989). New goals for teaching language: An experience in undergraduate programs in Spain. *Hispania, 72,* 774-779.

Sandarg, J., Schomber, J., & Wilkerson, C. (1999a, August). *Teacher certification and the Praxis II Exam.* Paper presented at the annual meeting of The American Association of Teachers of Spanish and Portuguese, Denver, CO.

Sandarg, J., Schomber, J., & Wilkerson, C. (1999b, November). *Preparing for Praxis II.* Paper presented at the annual meeting of The American Council on the Teaching of Foreign Languages, Dallas, TX.

Sandarg, J., & Wilkerson, C. (2002, September). *Strategies for success on the Praxis II Exam in Spanish.* Paper and workshop presented at the meeting of The Tennessee Foreign Language Teachers Association, Jackson, TN.

Sandarg, J., Wilkerson, C., & Riley, A. (2002, February). *Strategies for success on the Praxis II Exam in Spanish.* Paper and workshop presented at the meeting of The Foreign Language Association of Georgia, Athens, GA.

Sandrock, P. (1996). Changing the basis for articulation. *Hispania,79,* 545-547.

Stockwell, R., Martin, J., & Bowen, J. (1965). *The grammatical structures of English and Spanish.* Chicago: University of Chicago.

Sudzina, M. (2001). *"Psyching out" the "Praxis II test of learning and teaching": What our students need to know.* Paper presented at the Annual Meeting of the American Educational Research Association, Seattle, WA. (ERIC Document Reproduction Service No. ED 453 208)

Talburt, S., & Stewart, M. (1999) What's the subject of study abroad?: Race, gender, and "living culture." *The Modern Language Journal, 83,* 163-175.

Tannenbaum, R. (1994). *Defining the content domain for the Praxis II subject assessment in French: A job analysis focusing on knowledge and abilities.* Princeton, NJ: Educational Testing Service. (ERIC Document Reproduction Service No. ED 381 557)

Tannenbaum, R. (1992). *Job analysis of the knowledge and abilities important for newly licensed (certified) Spanish teachers.* Princeton, NJ: Educational Testing Service. (ERIC Document Reproduction Service No. ED 384 670)

5

The TPR Test: Total Physical Response as an Assessment Tool

Scott T. Grubbs
Valdosta State University

Abstract

The exigencies of producing students who are able to meet the demands of the global society have given second language study a new sense of purpose and importance among educators and policy-makers. Proficiency assessment, however, still relies heavily upon traditional discrete-item testing that focuses on grammatical structures and is often devoid of meaningful context. Total Physical Response (TPR), long a mainstay of foreign language instruction, has been frequently overlooked as a viable means for assessing proficiency. TPR is not only a valid means for gauging foreign language proficiency at increasingly complex levels, but it is capable of reinforcing core foreign language skills in a manner that appeals to students with various learning styles.

Introduction

In his 1966 article "The Learning Strategy of the Total Physical Response," James J. Asher, the psychologist credited with the development of the Total Physical Response (TPR) method of foreign language instruction, stated, "Perhaps one of the most complex tasks in human learning is the problem of how to achieve fluency in a foreign language" (p. 79). While this statement may strike foreign language practitioners as so self-evident as to beg discussion, the depth of the complexity of which Asher speaks is reflected in the frustrations and challenges that both teachers and students face while pursuing second language acquisition and proficiency. As Asher notes in a 2001(a) address to European educators:

> The evidence: 96% of students who voluntarily enroll in foreign language classes "give up" after three years. Only 4% continue to achieve at least minimal levels of fluency. More damaging: Not only do our students "give up" but they are now convinced that they "cannot learn another language." After all, they tried but the results were high-voltage stress and the humiliating experience of failure. (p. 1)

Although Asher was referring in this case to oral proficiency, it would not be out of the realm of logic to posit that the lack of foreign language proficiency also extended to aural, reading, and written skills as well. This lack of achievement and the high attrition rate among foreign language students become an even greater matter for concern as America moves into a new century in which increased economic, political, and cultural interdependence among nations has made foreign language acquisition an increasingly important and necessary part of American school curricula. The move to increase the curricular importance of foreign language instruction found favor not only among educators, but among policy-makers at state and national levels, as illustrated by the recommendations found in the education reform programs *A Nation at Risk* (National Commission on Excellence in Education, 1983) and *Goals 2000.* Indeed, as Nugent (2000) noted in her article, "Language Instruction in a Global Community":

> To be competitive in today's global economy, the business community has recognized the vital need for today's students and tomorrow's work force to be competent in languages other than English. Effective employees must be able to interact appropriately in face-to-face situations with those whose native language is not English. They must be able to interpret the concepts, ideas, and opinions expressed by members of non-English speaking societies through their art, literature, and media. (p. 38)

Moreover, during the 1990s, some states began to place increased emphasis on the importance of foreign language study, as illustrated by the observation in the overview to the *Massachusetts Foreign Language Curriculum Framework* (Massachusetts Department of Education, 1999) that "language is the medium in which human beings think and by which they express what they have thought. The study of language–any language–is therefore the study of everything that pertains to human nature, as humans understand it" (p. 1). Thus, in states such as Massachusetts, foreign language study has moved over the course of the last decade from an elective position in the school curriculum towards achieving a more prominent curricular status.

The Challenge of Foreign Language Assessment

At the same time that foreign language instruction was gaining increased recognition and acceptance as a central aspect of curriculum, American education witnessed an increased impetus towards accountability and assessment. This push for measuring student achievement through testing has most recently found expression in the mandates found in the *No Child Left Behind Act of 2001* and the education reform legislation enacted on state and local levels. While the majority of these efforts focus on language arts, mathematics, science, and social studies, there are efforts to hold foreign language teachers and students accountable for achievement in languages other than English. Currently, the National Center for Education Statistics (NCES) is preparing to field study the first Foreign Language National Assessment of Educational Progress (NAEP) for initial administration in the fall of

2004. The test, which will initially be offered in Spanish, will measure student performance in the areas of speaking, listening, reading, and writing (NCES, 2003). Additionally, foreign language achievement is assessed either directly in the form of state-mandated testing, such as the Regents' Spanish Test in New York (Zehr, 2003), or indirectly as a contributing indicator to overall school performance. In Georgia, for example, student achievement data on the foreign language advanced placement tests are included with scores from other advanced placement tests as part of the criteria to determine how well a school is meeting its educational objectives (Georgia Department of Education, 2003).

Despite the ever-increasing importance of foreign language assessment, serious concerns remain regarding the methods by which assessing achievement in second language acquisition is to be conducted. Educators recognize the importance that assessment plays in foreign language instruction and urge diversification in testing to include performance-based assessment, authentic materials, and evaluative techniques that encourage communicative approaches to measuring proficiency in the target language as opposed to an overriding emphasis on the memorization of grammatical structures (Massachusetts Department of Education, 1999). There is, nevertheless, still a great deal of reliance on the more traditional methods of foreign language assessment. These conventional strategies include criterion-based, teacher-made, discrete-point grammar assessments, vocabulary tests, and production-driven approaches to gauge oral proficiency (Asher, 2001b; Hall, 2001). As Hall notes, these types of traditional assessment are so prevalent because the primary foci in foreign language instruction are centered upon mastery of grammatical structures and vocabulary (p. 155). While these traditional assessment formats can play a valuable role in determining second language acquisition, overreliance on these methods can serve to undermine language proficiency and contradict the standards of foreign language learning as established by the profession in the mid-to-late 1990s, particularly those standards that address the ability to connect foreign language learning to other cultures, communities, and academic disciplines (National Standards in Foreign Language Education Project, 1999). Moreover, tests based on discrete-point grammatical items may serve to compromise language learning and usage in context by presenting the material to be tested in such a way as to become little more than a series of disconnected "non-sequiturs" (Omaggio, 1986).

Even in the instances when there is no disconnect between context and assessment, traditional methods of testing tend to favor those students who are most comfortable learning in the audio/visual modalities at the expense of those who learn primarily in other ways. As Howard Gardner, developer of the Multiple Intelligences Theory, observed in *Frames of Mind: The Theory of Multiple Intelligences* (1983):

> Yet it should be equally clear that current methods of assessing the intellect are not sufficiently well honed to allow assessment of an individual's potentials or achievements in navigating the stars, mastering a foreign tongue, or composing with a computer. The problem lies less in the technology of testing than in the ways in which we customarily think about the intellect and our ingrained views of intelligence. (p. 4)

Gardner (1983) formulated his theory of Multiple Intelligences to "challenge the classical view of intelligence that most of us have absorbed explicitly" (p. 5). He postulated that, rather than a singular conceptualization of intelligence, humans possess talents that can be classified as "intelligences" as long as these traits (1) have a developmental feature, (2) can be observed in special populations, (3) provide evidence of localization in the brain, and (4) can support a symbolic or notational system (Campbell, Campbell, & Dickinson, 1999). To this end, Gardner described, but did not limit himself to, eight intelligences: linguistic, logical-mathematical, spatial, bodily-kinesthetic, musical, interpersonal, intrapersonal, and naturalistic. These intelligences can be divided into sub-intelligences and are significantly influenced by the culture in which one lives and develops. While one may express aspects of more than one intelligence, Gardner maintains that one's creativity lies mainly within one domain of intelligence. Each of these intelligences has its respective developmental sequences and distinctive defining traits (Campbell, Campbell, & Dickinson, 1999). In the academic environment, students tend to learn more effectively when teachers ascertain the intelligences present in the classroom and pattern their lessons accordingly to meet the learning styles of their students.

Just as the theory of Multiple Intelligences has practical applications for classroom instruction, so does it possess the potential to provide more effective assessment of student performance. In particular, the theory encourages the use of authentic assessments so that students are able to express what they have learned in a meaningful context, an especially important aspect of second language proficiency assessment. Authentic, contextual assessments allow students to be evaluated through criterion-referencing, benchmarking, or ipsative means (Armstrong, 1994). Thus, foreign language teachers who incorporate the Multiple Intelligences concept into assessments that favor authentic, contextual assessments over traditional discrete-point, grammar-based tests may find that students previously at a disadvantage because of the audio/visual nature of traditional testing will demonstrate an increased level of content mastery. If, however, foreign language educators continue to rely on conventional assessment methods, those students who do not excel in the traditional testing formats will continue to experience a sense of heightened anxiety that may impede learning in the target language and reinforce negative student perceptions regarding foreign language acquisition (Asher, 2001b; Onwuegbuzie, Bailey, & Daley, 1999).

Total Physical Response

Although Asher is credited with the development of the Total Physical Response approach to foreign language acquisition, the method had its genesis in the work of Harold E. Palmer, an English advisor attached to the Japanese Ministry of Education, and his daughter, Dorothee, during the 1920s and 1930s. In *English through Action* (1925), Palmer and his daughter advanced the idea that second language acquisition was more effective in children when they carried out commands issued by the teacher in the target language. Palmer's work, however, received little notice outside Japan and subsequently fell into obscurity in the sociopolitical environment after World War II (Seely & Romijn, 2001)

The approach that practitioners have come to recognize as Total Physical Response began in the 1960s as an effort on the part of Asher, unaware of Palmer's work, to address the challenges facing foreign language pedagogy (Seely & Romijn, 2001). As Asher (1969) observed, "After studying a foreign language for two years, the average American not only has almost zero fluency, but negative learning may have resulted if the individual now has a fearful attitude towards second language learning" (p. 3). Asher reiterated the frustrations of conventional foreign language instruction in an address to the Alberta Teachers of English Conference in 2001, when he presented the all too familiar scenario of the teacher who "can ask students to practice an exercise for an hour, [and] come into the next class meeting and it is as if the exercise has been erased from the students' memories" (p. 2). It was Asher's initial contention that the foreign language curriculum was far too ambitious, given the amount of contact time allowed for instruction. Rather than attempt to attain proficiency in speaking, listening, reading, and writing, he posited that the first phase of foreign language instruction should focus on one skill, preferably listening, since listening proficiency has a high transferability to the other three language skills (Asher, 1969). Indeed, Asher's experimentation seemed to support Palmer's contention that action as a response to a spoken command facilitated second language acquisition; in Asher's specific case, this acquisition was expressed in terms of aural proficiency (Asher, 1966, 1969). Hence, the pedagogical method Asher proposed became known as *Total Physical Response* (TPR).

While subsequent refinements of TPR have included the advent of "TPR Storytelling" and a shift from an emphasis on primarily right-brain processes (Curtain & Pesola, 1994) to an increased focus on language learning activities utilizing both the left and right hemispheres of the brain (Asher, 2001c), the core principles of TPR have remained constant. As previously stated, the essential aspect of TPR has been the association of movement and language, often through an imperative delivery-active response format. Initially, the teacher models the command through several repetitions, consistently using the target language to identify the desired behavior. Once students respond to the command, the teacher then ceases to perform the target action, relying instead on the verbal expression of the imperative. Students do not undertake oral production until they feel sufficiently confident to make the effort, and stressors are kept to a minimum. Though initial instruction through TPR consists of short, basic commands, the level of complexity will increase in relation to the aural/oral proficiency of the students (Curtain & Pesola, 1994).

The reliance upon commands has led to three misconceptions regarding Total Physical Response: (1) TPR can be used only in conjunction with commands; (2) TPR has been effective only in the initial phases of foreign language instruction; and (3) TPR has been effective only with children (Asher, 2001d). In response, Asher (1996) noted that, while he placed much importance on command structures, the emphasis was on understanding as conveyed by the body movement of the students, allowing for the expansion of the Total Physical Response method to incorporate other grammatical and linguistic elements beyond the imperative mood. In terms of both instruction and assessment, the adoption of techniques like demonstration, natural dialogues, and TPR storytelling not only permitted usage beyond the realm of the command but demonstrated the efficacy of TPR in post-introductory levels of second language acquisition (Asher, 2001d; Seely & Romijn, 2001). As for the incorrect assumption that TPR has been effective only in instruction with young children, Asher's research (1969, 2001d) indicated that older language learners exposed to TPR actually outperformed younger students exposed to the same method. Thus, teachers who subscribed to these fallacies surrounding Total Physical Response assigned a nonexistent pedagogical rigidity to the method and subsequently denied their students an effective and vibrant means of foreign language instruction and assessment.

Assessment Strategies Using Total Physical Response

Assessment of Interpretive, Interpersonal, and Presentational Modes

Of all the core proficiencies in language learning, TPR techniques are most easily and directly applied in assessing listening comprehension. The strong relationship between oral production and bodily response that comprises the foundation of the Total Physical Response method allows the teacher to use TPR to evaluate how well students comprehend production in the target language according to how they respond to the teacher's output in the second language. Asher (2001a) referred to this process as the "language body conversation" (p. 9). Assessment via this strategy may be as simple as a game of "Simon Says," where the students respond appropriately according to the commands issued by the teacher. The evaluation of student progress is based on the number and complexity levels of the tasks they are asked to complete. As student comprehension and production increase, the assessment may be varied so that some students are giving instructions in the target language while others carry out the commands. In this case, the instructor evaluates the students according to how accurately the students give and respond to the commands issued during the test. Thus, the teacher would have the potential to evaluate student oral proficiency, as well as listening comprehension, at least on a basic level.

At more advanced levels, listening comprehension can be assessed through a variation of TPR Storytelling. In this format, the teacher would create a "mini-story" using the elements that are to be assessed. Students would act out the story based upon their interpretation of the events in the teacher's story. Assessment would be evaluated on the accuracy with which the student portrays the story. The advantage to this type of assessment is that it provides for evaluation of listening proficiency in longer, more complex linguistic structures within a given context, as opposed to the relatively basic assessment using short commands.

Another possible option using the TPR Storytelling strategy as a listening assessment is to have the teacher relate a story incorporating the material to be assessed. In this case, however, the students would draw a picture or a scene that depicts the teacher's story. Evaluation would be based upon the accuracy of the visual representation of the events in the story (Asher, 2001c). On the surface, this particular approach to assessment may not appear to conform to the format of classical TPR. The act of drawing, however, is actually a physical response to a linguistic stimulus, adding a kinesthetic dimension to the traditionally emphasized audio/visual approaches to foreign language instruction and assessment.

Seely & Romijn (2001) state that listening comprehension is such a fundamental element of Total Physical Response that this particular skill does not actually have to be assessed. In-class instruction using TPR provides the teacher with opportunities for informal assessment, but formally assessing listening proficiency allows teachers to determine whether or not the individual student actually comprehends output in the foreign language as opposed to merely mimicking the gestures of the other students. Moreover, current accountability trends in education put additional pressure on teachers to formalize areas of assessment that may have been previously evaluated in a satisfactory manner on an informal basis. Thus, foreign language instructors should be aware of the possibilities that TPR presents as a viable means of formally assessing listening proficiency.

Since oral proficiency is the language acquisition skill most closely associated with listening proficiency, it would not be unreasonable to suppose that oral proficiency assessment using Total Physical Response would be closely associated with the assessment strategies used to measure listening comprehension. A key aspect of oral production–and hence, assessment, in TPR–is a focus on "role reversal," in which the instructional emphasis in the second language shifts from the teacher's producing and demonstrating output to student production (Seely & Romijn, 2001). At the basic levels, students would effect the role reversal in simple command-response assessments discussed in the previous section on listening assessment, the difference being that the evaluative focus would be on oral production rather than on the response to the commands.

During subsequent phases of foreign language instruction, students may be assessed orally through the development of dialogues or mini-stories involving natural action dialogues and the TPR Storytelling method, strategies that allow the teacher to monitor student fluency in addition to the accuracy of oral production. When assessing through the natural action dialogues and TPR Storytelling, the teacher should clearly designate the words or structures that are to be assessed, and it is essential that the students have been previously exposed to the material in question. Moreover, while fluency should be monitored, it should not be the major evaluative priority. Rather, primary importance in oral assessment should be given to the comprehensibility of the student utterances.

Assessment of Presentational and Interpretive Modes

Although most closely associated with direct listening and oral assessment, Total Physical Response provides options for evaluating written and reading proficiency. To test writing skills, teachers may restructure the command-response assessment used for aural/oral assessment so that students respond to the teacher's physical stimuli in a written format, beginning with simple commands and progressing towards more complex structures as students become more competent in the target language.

Another means of measuring student achievement in writing is through TPR dictation (Seely & Romijn, 2001). In TPR dictation, the teacher models the items to be assessed through physical demonstration before orally presenting the sentence that is to be written by the students. Thus the item to be evaluated is presented through both kinesthetic and oral modalities. In using the TPR dictation, it is very important that the teacher refrain from using contexts and linguistic items that have yet to be formally presented in the instructional environment. Furthermore, the demonstrations must be free from ambiguity, and the oral delivery must be given clearly and at an appropriate conversational rate for the skill level of the students being tested. Other means of assessing writing include presenting students with pictures or images involving the material to be assessed and having the students write a passage or dialogue based on the visual stimulus and having them develop natural action dialogues in a written format (Seely & Romijn, 2001). These written dialogues can be used not only to assess written proficiency in the target language but also serve as a possible basis upon which to assess proficiency in both oral and reading skills.

As a result of the comparatively passive nature of reading, as opposed to listening, speaking, and writing, the assessment of reading proficiency through TPR may pose the greatest challenge to foreign language teachers. Evaluation of reading skills, however indirectly, is still possible through TPR, especially in the formats of the natural action dialogue and TPR Storytelling. Through these approaches, the student reads materials that cover the information to be tested, with either the teacher or the other students in the class acting out what the student reads. In an assessment situation, the stories and dialogues may be more effective if they are teacher-generated, but it would be quite feasible for students to create the dialogue or story (thus reinforcing writing proficiency). Role reversal plays an important part in reading assessment, as the students being evaluated are providing the stimulus, and the teacher or other nonevaluated members of the class are responding to what is being read. Students may be evaluated on criteria similar to those found in native-language reading instruction, including fluency, decoding skills, and comprehension, while being engaged in the assessment through an interactive format.

Potential Challenges to TPR Assessment

While Total Physical Response offers the foreign language instructor the means by which to assess students who learn in authentic contexts through a variety of intelligences, the strategy presents potential drawbacks if it is misused. If, for example, the context used to assess the target language were "bizarre" or overly strange, then language learning could be compromised because of the student's inability to manipulate the target language in an authentic situation, not to mention the context presented in the assessment (Omaggio, 1986). Omaggio even asserts that the greatest drawbacks to TPR derive from its "incongruence to proficiency goals" (p. 75). Indeed, some ideas and concepts are so abstract and difficult to present that they do not readily lend themselves to assessment through TPR. Additionally, some practitioners may find the indirect nature by which TPR assesses reading too problematic to be of practical value for use in the classroom. Overutilization of Total Physical Response may result in what has been termed "adaptation," whereby students cease to respond to the physical stimulus that underpins the TPR method (Seely & Romijn, 2001). Finally, some learners may find TPR to be exceedingly uncomfortable or embarrassing, not only hindering assessment but also adding to the type of anxiety that Asher wishes to avoid.

Conclusion

The issues involving context selection, proficiency challenges, adaptation, and student comfort level must certainly be taken into consideration when one employs the Total Physical Response method, not only as an assessment tool, but also as a pedagogical approach to foreign language instruction. Practitioners, however, need to remember that no one method of instruction or assessment will be completely effective with students in a foreign language course. As with instruction, the question facing foreign language teachers in dealing with assessment issues should not be which method to use in assessing students, but rather which combination of approaches will work best to effectively measure student achievement. When used in concert with other assessment techniques, Total Physical Response offers a dynamic and engaging means by which to test foreign language proficiency in authentic contexts across a range of student intelligences in such a way as to stimulate enthusiasm not just for a particular course or teacher, but for the desire to develop foreign language learning on a lifelong basis.

References

Armstrong, T. (1994). *Multiple intelligences in the classroom.* Alexandria, VA: Association for Supervision and Curriculum Development.

Asher, J. J. (1966). The learning strategy of the total physical response: A review. *The Modern Language Journal, 50,* 79-84.

Asher, J. J. (1969). The total physical response approach to second language learning. *The Modern Language Journal, 53,* 3-17.

Asher, J. J. (1996). *Learning another language through actions: The complete teacher's guidebook* (5th ed.). Los Gatos, CA: Sky Oaks.

Asher, J. J. (2001a). *Future directions for fast, stress-free learning on the right side of the brain.* Paper prepared for the International Association for Collaborative Contributions to Language Learning, Moscow, Russia. Retrieved January 4, 2004, from http://www.tpr-world.com/future.html

Asher, J. J. (2001b). *How the brain influences behavior.* Keynote address to the Alberta Teachers of English as a Second Language 2001 Conference, Alberta, Canada. Retrieved January 4, 2004, from http://www.tpr-world.com/calgarykeynote.html

Asher, J. J. (2001c). Learning another language through actions (6th ed.). Los Gatos, CA: Sky Oaks.

Asher, J. J. (2001d). *Some myths about TPR*. Retrieved January 4, 2004, from http://www.tpr-world.com/myths.html

Campbell, L., Campbell, B., & Dickinson, D. (1999). *Teaching & learning through multiple intelligences*. (2nd ed.). Boston: Allyn and Bacon.

Curtain, H., & Pesola, C. A. B. (1994). *Languages and children: Making the match: Foreign language instruction for an early start: Grades k-8 (*2nd ed.). White Plains, NY: Longman.

Gardner, H. (1983). *Frames of mind: The theory of multiple intelligences*. New York: Basic Books.

Georgia Department of Education. (2003). *2001-2002 Georgia education report card*. Retrieved January 4, 2004 from http://accountability.doe.k12.ga.us/Report02

Goals 2000: Educate America Act. PL 103-227. Retrieved January 4, 2004, from http://www.ncrel.org/sdrs/areas/issues/envrnmnt/stw/sw0goals.htm

Hall, J. K. (2001). *Methods for teaching foreign languages: Creating a community of learners in the classroom*. Upper Saddle River, NJ: Merrill Prentice Hall.

Massachusetts Department of Education. (1999). *Massachusetts foreign languages curriculum framework*. Malden, MA: The Commonwealth of Massachusetts Department of Education.Retrieved January 4, 2004, from http://www.doe.mass.edu/frameworks/foreign/1999.pdf

National Center for Education Statistics. (2003). *NAEP foreign language assessment*. Retrieved January 4, 2004, from http://nces.ed.gov/nationsreportcard/foreignlang/

National Commission on Excellence in Education (1983). *A nation at risk: The imperative for educational reform: A report to the nation and the Secretary of Education*. Washington, DC: U.S. Government Printing Office.

National Standards in Foreign Language Education Project (NSFLEP). (1999). *Standards for foreign language learning in the 21st century* (1999). Yonkers, NY: Author.

No Child Left Behind Act of 2001. PL107-110. Retrieved January 4, 2004, from http://www.ed.gov/policy/elsec/leg/esea02/index.html

Nugent, S. A. (2000). Language instruction in a global community. *NASSPBulletin, 84*, 35-40.

Omaggio, A. C. (1986). *Teaching language in context: Proficiency-oriented instruction*. Boston, MA: Heinle & Heinle.

Onwuegbuzie, A. J., Bailey, P., & Daley, C. E. (1999). Relationships between anxiety and achievement at three stages of learning a foreign language. *Perceptual and Motor Skills, 88*, 1085-1093.

Palmer, H., & Palmer, D. (1925). *English through actions*. Tokyo: Kaitakusha. (Reissued in 1955; slightly revised later edition, 1959. London: Longman).

Seely, C., & Romijn, E. K. (2001). *TPR is more than commands–at all levels* (2nd ed.). Berkeley, CA: Command Performance Language Institute.

Zehr, M.A. (2003). Schools tap talent for home languages. *Education Week, 22*, 22-23.

6

Assessing the Impact of Narrow Listening: Students' Perceptions and Performance

Victoria Rodrigo
Georgia State University

Abstract

Narrow listening (NL) is an approach to developing listening skills at intermediate to advanced levels. NL refers to listening to a single segment extensively and repeatedly for the purpose of meaning. The first part of this article reviews the listening material available in the foreign language setting and presents a case for introducing NL. It is followed by a study of students' perceptions of this approach and their performance on a listening comprehension test (N = 100). The results indicate that the practice of NL using audio library material is not only perceived as a useful and stimulating learning experience in acquiring Spanish but also proves to be an effective way to improve listening skills. Pedagogical implications are suggested.

Background

The literature in the field of first (L1) and second language (L2) acquisition greatly acknowledges the importance of good listening skills in language acquisition. Listening is the first language skill that humans develop: "As children, we listen before we speak, speak before we read, and read before we write" (Wolvin & Coakley, 1985, p. 7). In one's L2, listening also plays a crucial role and becomes a good predictor of success in the foreign language (Krashen, 2003). Consequently, having a good ability to understand the target language in its spoken modality should be a goal for any language student and FL program.

The present article reports on a study that assessed the impact of narrow listening (NL), an approach to developing listening skills at the intermediate and advanced levels (Rodrigo & Krashen, 1996), by analyzing students' perceptions of the approach and their performance on a listening comprehension test. For both studies, students' perceptions and performance, the subjects were drawn from fifth-semester courses based on a NL methodology. Additionally, for the perception study, the results of the NL approach were compared with those from courses with a traditional listening (TL) component (i.e., lab tapes accompanying textbooks in which the listening material is edited and, therefore, unauthentic). An explanation as to the reasons the NL was implemented must precede the report on these studies.

Does Listening Help?

Teachers are aware of the benefits of practicing listening comprehension (Berne, 1998) in order to improve L2, but are the students aware too? During the fall of 2000, a total of 203 college students of Spanish attending a lower-division language program (first through fourth semester) were asked to state whether the textbook tapes they were required to use for the practice of listening helped them acquire the target language. Table 1 shows their responses:

Table 1.
Students' opinions: Does listening help you acquire L2?

	Number of students	**Yes % (N)**	**No % (N)**
1 semester. TL	61	93 (57)	7 (4)
2 semester. TL	77	95 (73)	5 (4)
3 semester. TL	51	92 (47)	8 (4)
4 semester. TL	14	71 (10)	29 (4)

TL=traditional listening[1]

As Table 1 indicates, the students appear to value the listening material that language instructors make available to them and are aware of the benefits of practicing listening skills for the purpose of acquiring more Spanish. However, there is a slight difference between the first three semesters (with positive responses mostly at 92% and above) and the fourth-semester students (71%), who value their listening material less. This shift of opinion between the highly positive reactions in the first three semesters and those of the fourth semester certainly deserves attention. A possible reason could be a lack of effective, interesting, and appropriate material to practice this skill at the intermediate level (Campana, 1984). It is reasonable, then, to ask whether students in the fourth semester, now intermediate users of the target language, consider the listening material available to them to be (a) too easy and uninteresting or (b) too difficult, challenging, or frustrating. A review of the listening material available is therefore required.

A Gap Observed

The listening material currently used in FL teaching consists of tapes, CDs, and videos accompanying language textbooks, as well as culturally authentic audio material, such as media products (TV, videos, and radio). These material modalities differ from one another in both their characteristics and objectives. Textbook tapes, CDs, and videos generally expose language learners to edited, unauthentic language that is purely pedagogical in nature. Speakers read a script containing the vocabulary and grammar structures related to a particular topic in the textbook. Also, the speakers all too often sound unnatural, because they speak at a slow pace, and the language input typically conveys content that is not relevant to students.

Authentic material, by contrast, consists of natural, unedited language, and students are exposed to language input originally intended for a first language population. It is possible, then, that language learners are being forced to jump from scripted to authentic material without a proper transition. The apparent gap between the two modalities may explain why the fourth-semester students of the sample had a less positive view of the benefits that their listening activities might provide. Consequently, it is possible to conclude that an intermediate stage needs to be suggested in order to bridge the observed gap.

Bridging the Gap: Narrow Listening and the Audio Library

As a solution to the gap observed at the intermediate level, a three-stage model was proposed in the development of listening. The process consists of an initial stage, an intermediate (or transitional) stage, and a final stage. The transitional stage requires NL. Table 2 presents the pedagogical model proposed for developing listening skills in L2 (See Rodrigo, 2003, for more information about the pedagogical model and the theoretical foundations of NL.)

Table 2.
Pedagogical model for developing listening skills in L2 (from Rodrigo, 2003)

Stage	Text Characteristics	Material
Stage 1: Initiation	Unauthentic	Textbook tapes, CDs, and video
	Authentic	Video, audio with familiar and simple topics (i.e., commercials)
Stage 2: Transitional	Pedagogically authentic	Audio-library
	Authentic	TV, radio, and video (short or edited for length)
Stage 3: Final	Authentic	TV, radio, and video

The term NL, coined by Krashen (1996), refers to a relatively new concept in the field. NL is an approach to developing listening skills at intermediate-to-advanced levels. Four key questions explain the approach:

(1) Why listen? To get information, to know about a topic of interest.
(2) How to listen? Extensively, but at the same time, the listener must focus on a single topic and listen to the same passage as many times as needed, from beginning to end, without stopping the tape.
(3) What to listen to? Authentic speech samples of short duration (1 to 3 minutes) about a topic that is familiar and interesting to the listener.

(4) What to do? Activities that are relevant for the students. Based on the
speakers' information, students have to react to the content and express their opinions. The activities must allow different degrees of
understanding so that the students' level of anxiety can remain low.

NL, then, consists of listening to a single segment several times—as many as
the listener may need, an average of three to four times—for the purpose of com-
prehending the message the recorded speakers intend to convey. In a NL approach,
listening strategies are crucial for the success of NL activities. Language students
should know why and how to undertake NL activities. Therefore, they should be
made aware of the guidelines (Rodrigo, 1997) for an effective use of NL (see Appendix A).

Pedagogically Authentic Material: The Audio Library

Samples of NL material can be collected from TV, video, radio, or an audio
library. In the studies reviewed below, the subjects used a Spanish audio library. An
audio library is a sample of pedagogically authentic material, a new modality defined by Rodrigo (2003). Upon realizing that researchers had defined "authentic"
according to three separate factors: purpose (Geddes & White, 1978); source (Galloway, 1988); and quality of language (Rogers & Medley, 1988), Rodrigo combined
these factors into a definition of pedagogically authentic material as a "text produced by native speakers and used for a pedagogical purpose, for an L2 audience."
Such material contains language input that is natural and unmodified.[2]

The best example of pedagogically authentic material is an audio library used
in a narrow listening (NL) approach. Its main characteristics are as follows:

- *Material*: pedagogical, authentic, spontaneous, and brief
- *Length*: brief; between one and 3 minutes per passage
- *Focus*: general comprehension and practice on listening skills
- *Activities*: getting general information; reacting to the content
- *Topics*: of personal interest, since they are selected by the listeners
- *Strategy*: rehearing a single segment, extensive and narrow listening

The audio library used with the NL approach was a collection of three CDs
containing 25 topics of interest to the students. The topics were divided into four
categories: personal, speculative, controversial, and informational (see appendix B
for the list of topics). Three native speakers spoke freely and spontaneously about
their points of view or experiences related to each specific topic. The speech samples
were one-to-3-minute monologues. The Spanish audio library (Rodrigo, 2000) used
in the studies we will introduce included a total of 17 speakers from 10 Spanish-
speaking countries and more than 200 minutes of authentic, spontaneous input.
The students had access to the audio library in three ways. A set of the audio library

was available at the language lab, where students could listen to the segments or obtain copies for use at home. The students also had the option of purchasing the material. (The reader interested in how to create an audio library should consult Rodrigo, 2003.)

Study 1: Students' Perceptions on the Usefulness of NL in the Acquisition of Spanish

The data used in the analysis of students' perceptions on the effect of NL on their Spanish were collected in the fifth semester of college-level language study over a five-semester period (Spring'01 through Spring'03), and in six courses, with a total sample of 100 students. At the end of each semester, the students were asked to answer a questionnaire about several aspects of the NL approach. Three questions specifically addressed NL: (1) how the NL compared to other types of listening (e.g., lab tapes accompanying a textbook) the students had used before; (2) the students' perception about the usefulness of NL in improving their Spanish; and (3) areas in which and the degree to which NL was useful (see appendix C for questions used). Their answers follow:

A. How the NL compared to other types of listening

As a response to the first question, 81.8% of the students considered the practice of NL better than that for other types of listening material. The remaining 18.2% indicated that NL and listening activities in previous courses were about the same. No students considered the NL practice worse than traditional activities. Students reported that NL was considered better practice for listening comprehension because it was more interesting and not as monotonous as the lab tapes. The students' comments in the questionnaire revealed seven factors that, from their perspective, made NL more interesting than traditional listening. These factors, together with several illustrative comments, follow:

1. *Relevant topics*: The topics dealt with issues of current interest and debate that attracted the students' attention. Among their comments were these: "It's always better to listen to actual people talking about real topics." "NL included themes that I could relate to on a day-to-day basis, that went beyond a first-year Spanish level." "Focused on practical issues."

2. A *variety of speakers from different Hispanic countries*: "I like NL better because it offers various speakers with different accents and voices." "What I like the best about NL is becoming accustomed to different accents, hearing and understanding Spanish, and learning about different cultures, all at once." "There were many different speakers, and I liked to try and guess what country they were from."

3. *Natural language, like that in real life*: "NL is better because it gives you an opportunity to hear the language spoken in an unedited and close-to-natural environment. Also, you can hear different dialects." "The speakers are spontaneous, untrained, and real people speaking as they normally do." "[The language in NL

activities] is much more casual, informal; you can hear people speaking from all the different Hispanic countries." "They [the speakers] are real people, not actors who always speak perfectly." "[I like] the fact that the speakers don't use a script and speak the same as they speak in everyday life." "I appreciate the 'nativeness' of the speakers (not talking slow 'standard') even if they are really frustrating some-times." "I like the true life experience of speakers (did not understand everything though!)."

4. *Realistic and rewarding activities:* "NL is more realistic than classroom or the lab book. Workbook sheets don't feel like they accomplish anything." "I liked the fact that it was not made easy; the words used were not edited so we could understand."

5. *Personal learning experience:* The students are in charge of their own learning; they can choose what to hear (they select the topics), when, and where to do it (the listening activity was homework): "NL is more interesting because it is something I like doing. [It] allows you the possibility of listening to what you want to hear." "It was good to be able to do something like this on your own time and not in class with all the distractions." "I have to keep the tapes and listen to them as often as I want and when I want to." "There are different topics to choose from." "[I like] to listen to them at our own pace and the different dialects of speakers."

6. *First-hand target culture:* "This is educational, culturally as well as for grammar and comprehension." "It's more interesting and more educating about the culture and different types of accents." "I liked the way in which I learned about various Hispanic cultures as well as [the fact that I] listened to different accents and pronunciation of words."

7. *Makes it easier for the student to have a feeling of accomplishment:* "The more I listen to these tapes, the better I learn how to structure a conversation or just simple sentences." "You actually hear and try to comprehend how Spanish speak-ers actually speak." "Puts you in a total Spanish frame of mind." "Compared to doing lab book exercises that correspond to tapes, I like NL more." "I really en-joyed the activities, and I feel that they really helped me with my speaking, listening, and understanding. I feel like I have been internalizing Spanish a lot. . . . I really enjoyed the activities . . . because [they] helped me more than anything else!" "It helps me to understand people with different accents and speaking styles." "NL is concise and easy to understand." "I have never had something like NL and I think it is great."

In sum, the students felt that NL prepared them better to handle real L2: they were exposed to real people, a variety of accents and speaking styles, natural lan-guage, interesting topics, and relevant activities in a low-anxiety situation. At the same time the students enjoyed and liked working with NL. Some of the negative comments about NL were related to how fast some speakers spoke and about the sound quality of the recordings.

B. The students' perceptions about the usefulness of NL

A total of 95% of the students in the fifth semester responded that NL helped them acquire Spanish. This result is similar to the one observed in the first three semesters of the TL groups reported in Table 1. Table 3 clearly shows a decrease in positive responses during the fourth semester. It appears, however, that NL reinstated in the fifth semester the same value that the students had assigned to NL in the first three semesters. Table 3 shows the five-semester sequence:

Table 3.
Students' opinions. Does listening help you acquire L2?

	Number of students	Yes % (N)	No % (N)
1 semester. TL	61	93 (57)	7 (4)
2 semester. TL	77	95 (73)	5 (4)
3 semester. TL	51	92 (47)	8 (4)
4 semester. TL	14	71 (10)	29 (4)
5 semester. NL	100	95 (95)	5 (5)

TL = traditional listening; NL = narrow listening

C. Areas in which and the degree to which NL was useful

As for the third question, regarding the students' perception of the degree of usefulness of NL in the improvement of their Spanish in different areas, the students had to use a scale from 1 (not very useful) to 5 (very useful). Table 4 reveals the results:

Table 4.
Areas improved after using NL: Students' perceptions

Skills	*Number*	*Mean*	*SD*
Improving your **listening comprehension**	90	**4.52**	0.72
Knowing about another **culture** and different points of view	91	**4.26**	0.92
Improving your **communicative skills** in Spanish	89	3.81	1.08
Developing or reviewing your **vocabulary**	90	3.60	1.00
Improving your **fluency**	90	3.49	1.21
Improving your **pronunciation**	72	3.42	1.21
Getting used to **talking** in another language	89	3.39	1.36
Reviewing **grammar** structures in context	90	2.91	1.17

Table 4 indicates that NL, according to the students' perceptions, helped them the most in the areas of listening comprehension (4.52), followed by knowing about another culture (4.26), both rated as between "useful" and "very useful." Communication skills, vocabulary, fluency, pronunciation, and speaking received scores between "o.k." and "useful." Grammar attained the lowest rating, between "not useful" and "o.k."

Since study 2 focuses on the performance of these students on a listening test, it proves interesting to see in more detail the first question in Table 4 and compare the results of the NL and TL students. These results are reported in Table 5. A majority of the students, 61%, in the fifth semester, agreed that the NL material was very useful. Among the students in the first to fourth semesters who had used the more traditional textbook material, the positive tendency is clearly less marked (31.67%).

Table 5.
Improving your listening comprehension. Degree of usefulness according to students' perception. Traditional listening (TL) and narrow listening (NL)

	1 Not useful at all	2 Not useful	3 O.k.	4 Useful	5 Very useful
1-4 semester: TL N= 203	0 %	2.55%	23.75%	41.75%	31.67%
5 semester. NL N= 90	1.10 %	1.10%	3.30%	33.33%	**61.10%**

Consequently, it may be concluded that NL, as compared to the more traditional textbook material, was perceived very positively by the students. They considered the NL practice more beneficial, a perception that can certainly ensure higher levels of motivation. These results support the findings by Rodrigo and Krashen (1996) and Dupuy (1999). Thus, from the students' subjective point of view, NL has been shown to have a more significant effect on the learning process. A valid question at this point is whether the students' positive perceptions about NL relate in any way to better performance on listening tests.

Study 2: Students' Performance Using NL

In order to validate the students' perceptions, it is important to look at their performance and to determine whether their positive reactions to the NL material translated into improved listening skills. The data in study 2 were collected through a standardized listening test given at the beginning and at the end of each semester to the same population that participated in the perception study. NL was implemented by means of the audio library. The students were free to choose the more appealing topics of the audio library, and the activities were relevant and flexible, since they could be easily adapted to the students' level. Thus, the level of anxiety and frustration remained low.

The results of the t-test in Table 6 show that the scores were improved between the pre-test and post-test for all the groups and that these gains are statistically significant at different levels of probability. These results indicate that NL indeed helped the students improve their listening skills and that their positive perceptions had some foundation in reality.

Table 6.
Listening test results for NL groups: pre-test and post-test

Group	Pretest			Posttest		
	N	*Mean*	*SD*	*Mean*	*SD*	*t-test*
1	18	11.22	3.77	14	3.48	t(17)=-4.03, p<.001
2	19	10.78	3.69	14	3.85	t(18)=-4.89, p<.001
3	13	12.23	4.49	13.77	4.60	t(12)=-2.85,p<.05
4	14	11.64	4.22	15.07	3.22	t(13)=-7.81, p<.001
5	22	13.32	4.02	14.54	3.16	t(21)=-2.12,p<.05
6	14	14.64	3.48	16.78	3.12	t(14)—3.97,p<.01

Group 1: Spring'01   Group 2: Fall'01   Groups 3 and 4: Spring'02
Group 5: Fall'02   Group 6: Spring'03

Conclusion

The results for both studies, the students' perceptions and gain scores on a standardized listening test, strongly suggest that NL is an optimal tool for developing listening comprehension skills at the intermediate level and an adequate approach to maintain students' interest, motivation, and even self-confidence in their capacity to learn the L2. The implications of these findings are clear: The training in this language ability can be enhanced through the use of topics that are relevant and appealing to the students for listening material in which the language used is similar to what they will face in the real L2 setting (natural speech, different accents, and speaking styles) and to which they have had the chance to listen as many times as necessary. Also, students need to be exposed to listening material and activities that do not frustrate or bore them and that respond to their needs and expectations, so that they can experience a feeling of accomplishment that will motivate and encourage them to proceed with the mastery of the foreign language. As has been shown, NL restored at the intermediate level a positive perception of the practice of listening skill that by the fourth semester had begun to break down. NL appears to address the needs of students in the intermediate stage better than more traditional proposals.

Notes

[1]   Although there are fewer students in the fourth semester than in the previous three semesters, the decrease in positive responses cannot be ignored.

[2]   The audio library cannot be considered semiscripted material, or simulated authentic discourse (Geddes & White, 1978), as the speakers do not read a script or follow an outline in order to ensure the inclusion of particular vocabulary or grammatical features.

References

Berne, J. E. (1998). Examining the relationship between L2 listening research, pedagogical theory, and practice. *Foreign Language Annals, 31,* 169-190.

Campana, P. J. (1984). And now a word from our sponsor: Radio commercials for listening comprehension in German. *Unterrischtspraxis, 12,* 39-43.

Dupuy, B. (1999). Narrow listening: An alternative way to develop and enhance listening comprehension in students of French as a foreign language. *System, 27,* 351-361.

Galloway, V. (1998). Constructing cultural realities: "Facts" and frameworks of association. In J. Harper, M. Lively, & A.Williams (Eds.), *The coming of age of the profession* (pp. 129-140). Boston: Heinle & Heinle.

Geddes, M., & White, R. (1978). The use of semi-scripted simulated authentic speech in listening comprehension. *Audiovisual Language Journal, 16,* 137-145.

Krashen, S. (2003). *Explorations in language acquisition and use.* Portsmouth, NH: Heinemann.

Krashen, S. (1996). The case of narrow listening. *System, 24,* 97-100.

Rogers, C., & Medley, F. W. (1988). Language with a purpose: Using authentic material in the foreign language classroom. *Foreign Language Annals, 21,* 467-488.

Rodrigo, V. (2003). Narrow listening and audio library: The transitional stage in the process of developing listening comprehension in a foreign language. *Mextesol Journal: Mexican Association for English Teachers, 27,* 11-28.

Rodrigo, V. (2000). *Narrow listening.* Boston: Tomson Learning Custom Publishing.

Rodrigo, V. (1997, October). Narrow listening: A natural way to language development in the foreign language classroom. Fall Workshop for Foreign Language Teachers. *Louisiana Foreign Language Teaching Association (LFLTA).* Baton Rouge, LA.

Rodrigo, V., & Krashen, S. (1996). La audición enfocada en el aula y fuera de ella. *Greta, Revista para profesores de inglés, 4,* 71-75.

Wolvin, A., & Coakley, C. (1985) *Listening.* Dubuque, IA : Brown.

Appendix A

Criteria for Narrow Listening Activities

The effectiveness of narrow listening activities is ensured if all the following criteria are met:

1. The listening activity is for meaning, not form. Students want to listen to a passage because they are curious about what the speakers on the CD have to say. Students should concentrate on the speakers' ideas and comments.
2. The more frequently students listen to a particular segment, the more they will understand.
3. Students should not expect to understand every word the speakers say. Students need not stop the tape to listen again to a part they missed.
4. The listeners can listen to the CDs at their convenience–while driving, when out for a walk, before going to bed, and so forth.
5. The listening passages represent real situations, since native speakers talk spontaneously about their own experiences. These are not edited or graded conversations.
6. The listeners will be exposed to different accents (from Spain, North America, South America, and Central America) and different styles of speech.
7. The degree of difficulty will vary according to the topics and the speakers. Some speakers will be more comprehensible than others, some will be more talkative, and some will be more interesting. Certain topics will, of course, also prove to be more interesting than others.
8. Listeners should do the activity for themselves, for the improvement of their own communicative skills.
9. Listeners should not be discouraged if it is hard for them to understand a passage the first time; they should keep trying. It takes time to train one's ears to understand speech in another language. If the narrow listening segment is nearly completely incomprehensible, students should try another topic or another speaker.

How to Carry Out the Activity: Narrow Listening Guidelines for Students

As suggested by research on L2 listening, students should be given clear guide-lines as to how to complete narrow listening activities. These guidelines will ensure the success of the activity. Recommendations as to how students should complete a narrow listening activity include the following:

1. Select topics that are interesting or familiar to you.
2. Listen to one speaker at a time and listen to whole segments. Do not stop the CD until the speaker finishes talking (at least during the first two listenings). Try to get the gist of the speakers' accounts.

3. Replay a particular segment several times before proceeding. If a topic is interesting to you, listen to the other speakers who talk about the same topic. If it is not interesting, find another topic and follow the same procedure.
4. Move on to another speaker or topic if you understand almost everything, if you get to a point when you do not understand anything new, or if you are getting bored or tired.
5. The process of understanding is gradual. Research shows that students usually increasec their understanding of a listening passage by 10% each time they repeat it. At first, you will be able to recognize some words. Listen to the words surrounding those you recognize in order to discover new words and to understand sentences.
6. As you become more familiar with the activity and your auditory senses become accustomed to the Spanish language, you will understand more.

Appendix B

Spanish Audio Library

The audio-library contains 25 topics divided into four categories: personal, informational, speculative, and controversial.

Personal Topics: Audio CD 1

1. Descripciones personales: ¿Cómo eres? ¿Qué te gusta?
2. La familia: ¿Cómo es tu familia? ¿Qué hace?
3. Fin de semana típico: ¿Cómo es un fin de semana típico en tu vida?
4. De viaje: ¿Has viajado por el mundo? ¿Adónde has ido? ¿Qué has hecho?
5. La salud: ¿Tienes buena salud? ¿Haces algo para cuidarte?
6. Cine y televisión: ¿Te gustan?
7. La casa ideal: ¿Cómo es tu casa? ¿Cómo sería tu casa ideal?
8. La universidad: ¿Hay diferencias entre países? ¿Es igual en los Estados Unidos?
9. ¿Cómo te informas?: ¿Cómo te enteras de lo que pasa en el mundo?

Speculative Topics: Audio CD 2

10. Hombre / mujer ideal. Cita perfecta: ¿Crees que existen?
11. Vida en el futuro: ¿Cómo será la vida en el futuro?
12. El trabajo ideal: ¿Cómo sería tu trabajo ideal?
13. ¿Qué tres deseos le pedirías al genio Aladino?

Controversial Topics: Audio CD 2

14. La eutanasia: ¿Compasión o brutalidad?
15. Los toros: ¿Arte o barbarie?
16. Problemas del medio ambiente.
17. ¿Vida en otros planetas? : ¿Será verdad?

Informative Topics: Audio CD 3

18. Fiestas latinoamericanas
19. Choque cultural: lo diferente
20. Música: Argentina, España, y Chile
21. Papel de la mujer en la sociedad de hoy
22. Valores de la juventud
23. Fiestas de España
24. Valores de la familia
25. La comida: El Salvador, España, y Colombia. ¿Sabes cocinar...?

Appendix C

Questionnaire for Students' Perceptions

Note: Questions 1 to 3 were given to students using a NL approach. Only questions 2 and 3 were given to students using the TL approach. (For these latter items the NL questionnaire should read "narrow listening," and in the TL questionnaire should read "listening lab.")

1. How does Narrow Listening compare to other types of listening (e.g., lab tapes accompanying a textbook) that you have done before? Please, check one:

   ___ better   ___ about the same   ___ worse

   What did you like the best about Narrow Listening?

   What did you not like about Narrow Listening?

2. Do you think that, in general, the narrow listening/listening lab helped you improve your Spanish?   ___yes   ___no

3. If YES, check the following areas according to your own experience and the usefulness you think narrow listening/listening lab activities had in the improvement of your Spanish.

   1 = not useful at all;   5 = very useful

Improving your listening comprehension	1	2	3	4	5
Developing or reviewing your vocabulary	1	2	3	4	5
Reviewing grammar structures in context	1	2	3	4	5
Improving your fluency in Spanish	1	2	3	4	5
Getting used to talking in another language	1	2	3	4	5
Knowing more about another culture and different points of view	1	2	3	4	5
In general, improving your communicative skills in Spanish	1	2	3	4	5
Improving your pronunciation	1	2	3	4	5

4. If NO, please say why you think so.

7
Accounting for Activity:
Cognition and Oral Proficiency Assessment

Miguel Mantero
The University of Alabama

Abstract

Framing the present investigation within activity theory, this research analyzes the speaking guidelines of the American Council on the Teaching of Foreign Languages (ACTFL) and places the role of cognition and co-construction of meaning at the forefront of determining oral proficiency in a foreign language. Eight Spanish Oral Proficiency Interviews (OPIs) were analyzed in an effort to understand the overall role of cognition in developing and assessing oral proficiency. The findings are that although the ACTFL Proficiency Guidelines–Speaking *provide for an understanding of the various linguistic functions involved in speaking, they do not completely reflect the level of cognition evident during the OPI. Lastly, this article offers suggestions as to how to include the element of cognition within the construct of oral proficiency assessment as supported by instructional conversations and the concept of authentic assessment.*

Background

The purpose of this article is to analyze the aspect of cognition within the 1999 revised *Proficiency Guideline–Speaking* of the American Council on the Teaching of Foreign Languages (ACTFL) (Breiner-Sanders et al., 2000), and the Oral Proficiency Interview (OPI). The first phase of this study uses the *Florida Taxonomy of Cognitive Behavior (FTCB)*, established by Brown (1968) and further developed by Givens (1976), to describe the cognitive elements reflected in the *ACTFL Proficiency Guidelines*.

After the cognitive elements were identified, eight Spanish OPIs were transcribed, studied, and analyzed by means of the *FTCB*. The final step of this study compares the test-takers' observed cognitive behavior throughout the oral interviews to the elements of cognition identified by the *FTCB*.

This research is guided by the following essential questions:

1. To what extent is the element of cognition accounted for in the *ACTFL Proficiency Guidelines–Speaking* (Breiner-Sanders et al., 2000)?

2. To what extent is the cognitive behavior exhibited by the test-takers during the OPI reflected in the *FTCB* analysis of the *ACTFL Proficiency Guidelines*?
3. To what degree should the element of cognition shape our overall understanding of language learners' oral proficiency?

Teaching for Proficiency (or Competence?)

The field of language testing has a rich history (Bachman, 2000; Spolsky, 2000). The practical needs of language educators are a driving force behind many of its investigations and accomplishments. Teachers require that there be reliable and valid tools to assess individuals who are learning a second language. These evaluation instruments often influence how and what instructors teach in their classrooms (Clark, 1972; Liskin-Gasparro, 1984a).

The theoretical framework around which rubrics and tools are built may also help to structure whole curricula, as well as particular courses (Liskin-Gasparro, 1984b). Two definitions of "proficiency" are particularly interesting:

*   "Proficiency equals achievement . . . plus functional evidence of internalized strategies for creativity expressed in a single global rating of general language ability over a wide range of functions and topics at any given level" (Lowe, 1988, p. 12).
*   "[Proficiency is] the technical ability to use a foreign language without noticeable accent or grammatical errors" (Sollenberger, 1978, p. 8).

One may be able to transform the above statements into course goals to which clear, discrete objectives are then later added.

However, there are critics of "proficiency-driven" curricula and oral proficiency testing (Savignon, 1972; Bachman & Savignon, 1978; Lantolf & Frawley, 1985). Initially stemming from the support for the construct of communicative competence (Savignon, 1972), the "anti-proficiency movement" is now focused on the lack of attention that rubrics like the OPI give to the sociolinguistic and sociocultural factors involved in second language learning and successful oral communication (Barnwell, 1989). Given these insights, the present investigation hopes to continue the debate reflected in the following question: To what degree should language educators permit proficiency-based rubrics to influence their teaching and assessment methods?

Cognition and Language

The primary role of language is to give us enough information to interpret the reality of our particular world so that we are able to interact successfully in various communities of practice. In other words, as Neisser (1976) states, language allows for the acquisition, organization, and application of knowledge. Moreover, cognitive activity (thinking) shapes language according to our initial perceptions of reality.

To communicate, speakers must understand one another's intentions with respect to the context.

It is in communities of inquiry and participation that we learn how to co-construct meaning through dialogue embedded in goal-directed action (Lantolf, 2000; Wells and Claxton, 2002). However, linguistic interaction does not necessarily entail a dialogue. In order for dialogue to take place, participants must be involved in knowledge construction that surpasses linguistic coherence and relies on conceptual (cognitive) cohesion. That is, one does not necessarily need to speak more if he or she is familiar with a situation that is being discussed (Coulthard, 1977: Hagen, 1990). Such is the case with native speakers.

Native speakers are specialists in understanding the reality of a situation and therefore use language as effortlessly and as little as possible because language is a tool of thought. Nonnative speakers are more apt to focus on linguistic coherence (especially syntactic elements) because they view language as skill to be demonstrated and displayed to others (Barnwell, 1989).

Methodology: Cognitive Analysis of the OPI and Test-Taker Utterances

The individuals who took part in the OPIs were students in a third-semester, university-level Spanish class in Ohio: 5 males and 3 females. Eight OPI interviews were audiotaped, transcribed, and analyzed through the use of the *FTCB*. After completing the *FTCB* analysis, the researcher asked for the outcome of the OPIs and then compared the elements of cognition evident in the level descriptors with the language used by the test-takers throughout the actual OPI.

The examiner is a native speaker of Spanish who is ACTFL/OPI certified. Neither the tester nor the test-takers were shown the *FTCB* before any of the eight interviews. The individual interviews generally took 20-25 minutes each in accordance with the following process:

> [Through a] series of personalized questions . . . the interviewer elicits from the test candidate examples of his or her ability to handle the communication tasks specified for each level of proficiency in order to establish a clear "floor" and "ceiling" of consistent functional ability. Often candidates are asked to take part in a role-play. This task provides the opportunity for linguistic functions not easily elicited through the conversational format. (American Council on the Teaching of Foreign Languages, 2003)

The Florida Taxonomy of Cognitive Behavior

The OPI speaking scales were analyzed by means of Brown's (1968) and Givens's (1976) *Florida Taxonomy of Cognitive Behavior* (*FTCB*), which is based on Bloom's (1956) *Taxonomy of Educational Objectives*. It is important to note that Vygotsky's (1978) concept of mental functions is similar to that included by Bloom (1956) in his taxonomy of cognitive functions and also appears in the *FTCB*. The one element that is central to these three interpretations of cognition is language, because it facilitates the acquisition of cognitive skills and higher mental functions.

According to Webb (1970), the *FTCB* makes the hypothesis that just because intellectual abilities become increasingly complex in nature, one may not conclude that the higher levels are present only in the cognitive behavior of mature individuals or those with advanced linguistic proficiency. Rather, they can occur at each developmental stage, although in a different form. In other words, a low level of language proficiency does not necessarily entail a low level of cognitive ability. Moreover, both cognitive and linguistic development involve the acquisition of both knowledge and language and their utilization.

According to Brown (1968) and Givens (1976), there are seven increasingly complex areas of cognitive behavior and 55 levels that fall within these areas in the *FTCB*. In line with the initial thoughts of Bloom (1956), the seven main areas within the *FTCB* are as follows:

1. *Knowledge (levels 1-17):*
    This area makes up about one-third of the total items on the *FTCB* and has been subdivided into two categories: (a) *Knowledge of specifics* (levels 1-13), and (b) *Knowledge of universals and abstractions* (levels 14-17). The cognitive behaviors in levels 1-17 are all memory-based. That is, the individual does not have to take into account new information to take part in communication.

2. *Translation (levels 18-23):*
    This area is self-explanatory; however, one should realize that this section may entail cognitive behavior expressed in either language.

3. *Interpretation (levels 24-29):*
    Here one understands how ideas are interrelated.

In areas 4-7, individuals must use the knowledge they possess or to which they have recently been exposed.

4. *Application (levels 30-32):*
    A person must know the information well enough to be able to use it in a new situation.

5. *Analysis (levels 34-44):*
    These levels emphasize the relationship and the organization of the elements of communication and discourse.

6. *Synthesis (levels 45-53):*
    Within this area a pattern of communication emerges that is unique to the situation and participants.

7. *Evaluation (levels 54-55):*
    Here, the participants consciously judge and evaluate the information presented.

External Investigator and Transcription Conventions

This study made use of an external investigator who held ACTFL/OPI certification in Spanish. The tester was not the same one who administered the OPI to the students. After the external investigator was trained to interpret the *FTCB*, the primary researcher and the external investigator analyzed the linguistic and communicative functions described within each of the OPI level descriptors included in the *ACTFL Proficiency Guidelines–Speaking*. Using the *FTCB*, the external investigator also analyzed the eight student OPIs.

The primary researcher and the external investigator then compared their notes and their results of the analysis based on the *FTCB* analysis of the ACTFL guidelines and the eight interviews. Lincoln and Guba's (1985) formula to compute the reliability of the inter-rater agreement in analysis of both the ACTFL guidelines and the eight interviews was then implemented. The formula takes into account the overall truth value, applicability, consistency, and neutrality of the analysis. Accordingly, the inter-rater agreement for the *FTCB*-OPI guidelines analysis was computed at 94.1%. The inter-rater agreement for the eight OPI tests and the discourse analysis was computed at 90.3%. An analysis of these figures reveals an average inter-rater agreement of 92.2%

The researcher and the external investigator did not attempt to assign cognitive behavior to a speaking level if there was no word or phrase in the descriptor that clearly established a cognitive behavior. Therefore, about 36% of cognitive functions in the *FTCB* appear to have no linguistic counterpart in the OPI descriptors/guidelines.

The OPIs were transcribed according to the following transcription conventions developed and used by Brown and Yule (1981) and Johnson (1995):

+	indicates a pause
++	indicates a longer pause
//	indicates that two speakers start simultaneously
/	indicates that the next speaker overlaps at this point
*	indicates where the overlap ends
< >	indicates that the translation is not direct and denotes meaning rather than a word-for-word translation.

Data Analysis: Samples from OPI Interviews

The following interactions took place between the student (S) and the interviewer (I) during the sessions previously described. It is important to note that the following samples form part of a larger set of data. However, they demonstrate the overall pattern of talk that took place during the OPIs, and they bring to the forefront the central topic of cognition and oral language assessment. The primary researcher and the external investigator were in complete agreement as to the analysis of the following exchanges.

In the first illustration, the student and the interviewer are role-playing "two friends making plans for the weekend." The student is an American male whose family members do not speak Spanish. This exchange took place towards the middle of the interview.

Exchange #1

1. I: ¿Vas a estar en casa este fin de semana? *(Are you going to be home this weekend?)*
2. S: Sí.++ *(Yes)*
3. I: Vale.+ Entonces vamos a cenar en el nuevo restaurante el domingo. *(O.k. Then let's have dinner at the new restaurant on Sunday.)*
4. S: No poder. ++ Quiero // ver mi padre domingo. *(No, <I can't>. I want to see my father on Sunday.)*
5. I: // Entonces, ¿por qué no vamos al cine el sábado? *(Then why don't we go to the movies Saturday?)*
6. S: Él vive + en Atlanta. Estoy en el coche 10 horas. *(He lives in Atlanta. I am in the car 10 hours.)*
7. I: Ahhhhhh, + así que sales para casa, para Atlanta, el viernes. *(Ahhhhhh, so you leave for home, for Atlanta, on Friday.)*
8. S: No ++ jueves. *(No . . . Thursday)*
9. I: Vale, vale. *(O.k., o.k.)*

The interviewer rated the student's oral proficiency at Intermediate Low. The *ACTFL Proficiency Guidelines* (Breiner-Sanders et al., 2000) describe "Intermediate-Low" level proficiency as:

> Creating with language in straightforward social situations. Concrete, direct. Predictable. Reactive. Asking a few appropriate questions. Ineffective reformulations and self-corrections. Ability to order food or make purchases.

Exchange #1 reflects some of the linguistic functions expressed in the guidelines. The student's utterances were then analyzed using the *FTCB*.

Turn 2. *FTCB* levels 5 and 24: gives a specific fact and gives reason
Turn 4. *FTCB* level 27: shows cause-and-effect relationship
Turn 6. *FTCB* level 39: points out particulars to justify conclusion
Turn 8. *FTCB* level 42: detects error in thinking

According to the analysis of the *ACTFL Proficiency Guidelines*, "Intermediate Low" proficiency involves the cognitive behavior exhibited by the student in turns 4, 6, and 8. Although there were some grammatical errors in the student's utterances and the pronunciation was not "native-like," the student was able to use language to communicate his plans for the weekend. But, more importantly, at the beginning of the dialogue the interviewer thought that "home" meant the student's apartment in Ohio; however, by the end of the exchange the student was able to convey his meaning of "home" (Atlanta) to the interviewer (turn 7).

The student in Exchange #2 has Spanish-speaking parents, but she was born in the United States. The student's home language is English, but every now and then she speaks to her parents in Spanish, "a sentence at a time." This conversation occurs towards the end of the interview, yet it exemplifies the overall pattern of discourse and length of utterances used by the student. The subject matter is the purpose of homework, reading, and speaking.

Exchange #2
1. I: Bueno ++ para mí + es importante leer y escribir mucho. (*Well, for me, a lot of reading and writing is important.*)
2. S: No creo ++ Escribimos en clase mucho ++ y // leer. (*I do not think so. We write a lot in class . . . and < read>.*)
3. I: // Pero en clase hablamos mucho ++ ¿no? Si hablamos mucho ++ no hay tiempo para leer y escribir. (*But, we talk a lot in class, <right>? If we talk a lot . . . there is no time for reading and writing.*)
4. S: ++ Hablamos en la lectura. (*We talk <about> the reading.*)
5. I: Claro ++ pero// (*Of course, but*)
6. S: // Es diferente. (It is different)
7. I: ++Diferente ++¿cómo ? *(Different, how?)*
8. S: Me gusta hablar ++ de otra tema. (*I like to talk about <other things>.*)
9. I: + No entiendo. (*I don't understand.*)
10. S: Leer es de ++ como memoria / (*Reading is from++ like memory.*)
11. I: / ¿ y hablar?* *(And speaking?)*
12. S: Diferente ++ otra idea, no en libro. (*Different . . . another idea, not in <the book>.*)
13. I: Entonces no te gusta hablar de la tarea. (*Then you don't like to talk about the homework.*)
14. S: ++ Sólo mi idea. *(Only my idea)*

The interviewer rated the student in Exchange #2 as "Intermediate-Mid." The *ACTFL Proficiency Guidelines* (Breiner-Sanders et al., 2000) describe an "Intermediate-Mid" level speaker as:

> [Able to] perform a variety of uncomplicated tasks. Predictable and concrete exchanges. Reactive. [Has] difficulty linking ideas, using communicative strategies, manipulating time and aspect. [Able to] create with language for personal meaning. [Producing] utterances of sentence length, and some strings of sentences.

Exchange #2 reflects some of the linguistic functions described as "Intermediate-Mid." The following test-taker utterances in Exchange #2 were analyzed using the *FTCB*:

Turn 2.   *FTCB* levels 5 and 26: gives a specific fact; and summarizes, concludes from observation of evidence

Turn 4.   *FTCB* level 37: points out unstated assumption

Turn 6.   *FTCB* level 54: evaluates something from evidence

Turn 8.   *FTCB* level 39: points out particulars to justify conclusion

Turn 10.   *FTCB* level 28: gives analogy, simile, and metaphor

Turn 12.   *FTCB* level 46: produces unique comment, divergent idea

Turn 14.   *FTCB* level 5: gives a specific fact

Most of the linguistic functions described under "Intermediate-Mid" do not address the cognitive behavior observed in the student's utterances in Exchange #2. The primary researcher and the external investigator noticed that the cognitive elements in utterances 2, 4, 6, 8, and 10 are not accounted for in the "Intermediate-Mid" proficiency descriptors. It was noted that of the eight students whose interviews were analyzed, this one was the most willing to communicate. The interviewer suggested that such willingness may have resulted from her home environment. As in Exchange #1, the interviewer and student had to co-construct the meaning of a particular concept. In Exchange #2, the pair had to try to perceive each other's understanding of "speaking in class." The transcript also indicates that the student believes that speaking/classroom talk should not be about the reading, but the interviewer, who is also her teacher, believes that one of the main purposes of the readings is to provide a framework for discussions. Such activity hinges much more on the cognitive adaptation of the meaning of "speaking in class" than it does on the linguistic functions uttered by the interlocutors.

The following dialogue occurred with a female student who had spent two summers in Spain as part of a study-abroad program. This discussion occurred 10 minutes into the interview and revolves around the role-play, "Plans for next summer":

Exchange #3
1.   S: No quiero estar aquí. (*I don't want to be here.*)
2.   I: ++Pero si te quedas puedes ahorrar // dinero. (*But if you stay, you can save money.*)
3.   S: // Quiero volver a Sevilla. (*I want to go back to Sevilla.*)
4.   I: Pero no tenemos dinero. ¿Qué le vamos a hacer? (*But, we don't have money.* < *What are we going to do?*>)
5.   S: ¡Trabajad más! Y yo ++ mucho más. (*Work more!* <*Me too*>, *much more.*)
6.   I: ¿Cómo? Tienes que estudiar, / ¿no? (*How? You have to study,* <*right*>?)
7.   S: / Un poco * ++ Soy inteligente. Habla con papa, ¿vale? + ¡Tiene mucho dinero! (*A little . . . I am intelligent. Talk to dad, OK? He has a lot of money!*)
8.   I: Pero + tiene que pagar los impuestos. (But, he has to pay taxes.)

9.   S: Que ++ ¿repite, por favor? (*What, please repeat?*)
10. I: + ¡El IRS! Así que no hay dinero + // para viajar. *(The IRS! So there isn't any money for travel.)*
11. S: // Sí hay ++ ¡Que no paga la IRS! Puedo ir + entonces. *(Yes, there is <Don't pay> the IRS. Then <I'll be able to go>.)*

The interviewer rated this student as "Advanced-Low." According to the *ACTFL Proficiency Guidelines* (Breiner-Sanders et al. 2000), a speaker with Advanced-Low proficiency

> [Can] narrate and describe in all major time frames. Rephrasing. Participates actively. Circumlocution. Combine and Connect discourse. Single paragraph utterances. False cognates. Literal translation. Linguistic quality and quantity deteriorate significantly [if attempt to communicate is made beyond this level].

The following test-taker utterances in Exchange #3 were analyzed by means of the *FTCB*:

Turn 1.   *FTCB* level 5: gives a specific fact
Turn 3.   *FTCB* level 5: gives a specific fact
Turn 5.   *FTCB* levels 53 and 54: draws inductive generalization from specifics and evaluates something from evidence
Turn 7.   *FTCB* levels 47 and 42: produces a plan or a proposed set of opportunities and detects error in thinking
Turn 9.   *FTCB* level 31: applies principle to new situation
Turn 11.   *FTCB* levels 34, 47, and 39: distinguishes fact from opinion, produces a plan or a proposed set of opportunities, and points out particulars to justify conclusion

Of the cognitive behavior exhibited by the student in Exchange #3, only levels 5 and 31 of the *FTCB* fall within the "Advanced-Low" guidelines. According to the analysis, the other 6 cognitive functions in Exchange #3 are not addressed within the descriptors. From the dialogue, it is evident that the interviewer understood the rationale behind the student's solution to not being able to afford to travel to Spain. Interestingly, the student used the information provided (there is money for the IRS) in order to convince her "mother." This dialogue exemplifies what was found to be true throughout all of the interviews. That is, the complexity of thought observed is much more than the level of linguistic difficulty apparent in all eight of the OPIs studied.

Exchange #4 revolves around the topic of weather. The student is a non-native speaker of Spanish but is married to a graduate student from Guatemala. The following conversation took place a few minutes into the interview after the tester commented that it had been a very cold winter:

Exchange #4

1. S: Sí + y mi esposo no gusta frío. (*Yes, and my husband doesn't like <the cold>.*)
2. I: Pero, ¿no hace frío // en Guatemala? (*But, isn't it cold in Guatemala?*)
3. S: // No. Nunca hace frío ++ Hace más frío aquí en Ohio. ¡Mucho! (*No. It is never cold. It is colder here in Ohio. Much <more>!*)
4. I: Entonces, dime ++ ¿Cómo te gusta el verano en Ohio? + Están más a gustos en junio y julio, // ¿Verdad? (*Then tell me. . . . How do you like the summertime in Ohio? You are more comfortable in June and July, right?*)
5. S: // Sí y no ++ El verano es ++ está bien. Comfortable, sabes? Pero + el temperatura no me importa. Es que no hay amigos aquí. No tenemos dinero por viajes ++ nosotros quedamos en (Ohio). Sin frío + pero no con amigo. En el frío tengo amigos. (*Yes and no. The summer is . . . <it's> o.k Comfortable, you know? But the temperature doesn't matter. <It's that> there aren't any friends here. We don't have money <to travel>. . . we stay <here>. <Not cold, but without friends. When it's cold, we have friends>.*)

The interviewer rated this student at the "Advanced-Low" level as well. According to the analysis, some of the *FTCB* functions displayed by the student responses (25, 27, and 39) are not taken into account by the current OPI rubric.

The following test-taker utterances in Exchange #4 were analyzed using the *FTCB*:

Turn 1.   *FTCB* level 5: gives a specific fact
Turn 3.   *FTCB* levels 5 and 25: gives a specific fact, and shows similarities, differences
Turn 5.   *FTCB* levels 5, 27, 38, 39, and 46: gives a specific fact, shows cause-and-effect relationship, shows interaction or relation of elements, points out particulars to justify a conclusion, and produces a unique comment, divergent idea

The student's overall pronunciation, intonation, and pace of interaction were better than those of most of the other students. After the researcher transcribed the eight OPIs, he asked the rater to pick out what she considered to be "paragraph-length" utterances as proposed by the guidelines under Advanced-Low. Of all of the OPIs that were analyzed and transcribed, the above sample is the one that the rater considered to contain "paragraph-length" utterances (turn 5). However, the rater mentioned that when she attempted to linguistically guide the student's responses a little more, the student began to speak in shorter utterances.

The fifth student has followed the "traditional" foreign language curriculum of study–2 years of high school Spanish–and now will take 2 years (four semesters) of study at the college level. He has never spent any time in a Spanish-speaking country and does not have Spanish-speaking family members or acquaintances. The following interaction occurred 15 minutes into the interview about the topic "Studying for a biology exam":

Exchange #5

1. I: ¿No estás preocupado? + Has estudiado mucho este semestre. *(You aren't worried? You have studied a lot this semester.)*
2. S: Estudio mucho ++ Más que el otro clase. *(I study a lot. More than the other class.)*
3. I: Entonces el examen será muy fácil, ¿verdad? Y sacarás una "A" en // la clase. *(Then the exam will be very easy, <right>? And you'll get an "A" in the class.)*
4. S: // No sé ++ El examen es fácil + pero la clase es difícil. Tengo una "C" // en la clase. *(I don't know. The exam is easy, but the class is difficult. I have a "C" in the class.)*
5. I: // ¿Cómo? + No entiendo. *(How? I don't understand.)*
6. S: ++ En clase tengo ++ "lab." *(In class I have lab).*
7. I: ¿Para qué es + "lab"? (What is lab for?)
8. S: ++ Experimentar. No me gusta lab y es mucho parte de grado. *Experiment. I don't like lab and <it is a big part of our grade>.)*
9. I: ++ ¿Cómo podrías prepararte mejor // para el laboratorio? *(How could you better prepare yourself for the lab?)*
10. S: // No sé. Español es más mejor. No penso.++ // Es memorizar. *(I don't know. Spanish<is better>. I don't think. <It is only memorization>.)*
11. I: // ¡No piensas en español! *(You don't think in Spanish!)*
12. S: ++ No. Sólo verbos y vocabulario ++ es como diccionario. *(No. Only verbs and vocabulary . . . like a dictionary.)*

The interviewer rated this student's oral proficiency as "Intermediate-Mid." According to the OPI guidelines (Breiner-Sanders et al., 2000), "Intermediate-Mid" level speakers are described as:

[Able to participate in a] variety of uncomplicated tasks. [Able to participate in] predictable and concrete exchanges. Reactive. [Have] difficulty linking ideas and using communicative strategies. [Can] create with language for personal meaning. [Use] utterances of sentence length, and some strings of sentences.

The following test-taker utterances in Dialogue #5 were analyzed using the *FTCB*:

Turn 2.   *FTCB* levels 5 and 25: gives a specific fact and shows similarities, differences

Turn 4.   *FTCB* level 5 and 26: gives a specific fact; summarizes, concludes from evidence

Turn 6.   *FTCB* level 39: points out particulars to justify conclusion

Turn 8.   *FTCB* levels 5 and 24: gives a specific fact and tells why

Turn 10.   *FTCB* levels 5, 54, and 26: gives a specific fact, evaluates, and summarizes from evidence

Turn 12.   *FTCB* level 28: gives analogy, simile, and metaphor

Only levels 5 and 24 of the *FTCB* fall within the "Intermediate-Mid" guidelines. The others are not addressed within the descriptors. Although, according to the rater, the student's pronunciation and knowledge and use of grammar throughout his OPI were rather poor, he was able to communicate general ideas. More importantly, the student was able to explain and support his views about how his biology grade is generally determined.

Evident in the descriptors of the speaking levels and the interview process is the realization that the OPI does not account for how the person learned to speak. As noted by ACTFL (2003), the interview focuses on a person's "functional speaking ability, independent of any specific curriculum [because] it is irrelevant when, where, why, and under what conditions the candidate acquired his/her speaking ability in the language" (p. 1).

Here it seems that it is the display of linguistic skill that is being measured rather than the use of language in order to meet communicative goals. Evaluating communication entails measuring understanding, comprehension, and cognition. If the issue of cognition in the above instances challenges our interpretations of "proficiency," then it becomes much more complicated when we engage individuals in extended language use, where meaning emerges as a driving force behind communication. Somehow, as demonstrated by the comments in turns 10 and 12 of Exchange #5, a person's learning environment needs to be accounted for, because it affects how one uses language and the appropriate learning strategies.

Measuring Proficient Minds

The present study explores the construct of oral proficiency as presented by the *ACTFL Proficiency Guidelines— Speaking*. After the ACTFL level-descriptors were studied using the *FTCB*, the test-takers' actual language use was evaluated and compared to the initial understanding of cognition reflected in the *FTCB*. Space limitations do not permit inclusion of the complete OPI transcriptions. However, it is interesting to note that about 46% of all of the test-taker utterances did not fit within the cognitive expectations delineated by the *Proficiency Guidelines*.

The other three students tested were rated "Intermediate-Low," and all took part in some type of role-play during the OPI. The average student utterance (in all eight OPIs) was about 10 words. After careful analysis, it was determined that the main task of the test-taker utterances was to develop an understanding of the views, arguments, and reasoning that motivated language use in the first place, rather than just the performance of a "linguistic function." This last realization was particularly surprising because the researcher expected the OPIs to be much more reliant on linguistic coherence. However, the rater later noted that during the role-plays many students interpreted "linguistically focused" attempts as calling for something other than what was being discussed. In other words, when the interviewer attempted to guide the test-taker's utterances linguistically, rather than conceptually, the pace and quality of discourse suffered as the result of a loss of cohesion and lack of communication. This observation may be attributed to the type of training the interviewer received or to how she put her training into practice. As Brown (2003) points out, there is a great deal of interviewer variation during oral proficiency assessment.

Although individuals may receive exemplary training, the interviewer's technique may very well affect the test-taker's performance. Bachman (1990) attributed the problem of interviewer variation to an "inability to provide clear and unambiguous theoretical definitions of the abilities that we want to measure" (p. 50). Bachman's conclusion may partially explain the difficulty of researching the effects of cognition on oral proficiency or communicative competence in a second language. How can we then account for the element of cognition in second language learners' oral proficiency?

There needs to be more research on the role and place of cognition and how it affects one's overall oral proficiency in another language. As demonstrated by this investigation, the rubrics that the fields of language education and second language acquisition are accustomed to using across the disciplines may be an initial focus of inquiry. Here follow some suggestions as to how to include and account for the construct of cognition within oral proficiency assessment:

Instructional Conversation, Authentic Assessment, and Indigenous Assessment

As previously mentioned, one aspect that has yet to be elaborated on is the effect that the interviewer has on the language spoken by the test-taker. It is clear that the interviewer in this study knows the test-takers well because she is their teacher. The teacher/evaluator referred to common frames of reference throughout the OPIs and later suggested that this may be a reason why the students interacted well with her.

Both Barnwell (1989) and Hagen (1990) question the roles of the interviewer and their effect on the overall OPI assessment. It is suggested that the interviewer affects linguistic interaction and emerging speech. Moreover, as demonstrated by this study, when one assesses another's language ability, it becomes necessary to address the action that engages the individual in language learning rather than the constructs that define linguistic structures. Examples of such constructs are the T-unit or fragment (Chaudron, 1988). Wiggins (1990) and Archibald and Newman (1989) refer to evaluation that addresses the action that engages the individual as *authentic assessment*, as summarized by Mantero (2002b):

Authentic Assessment requires students to demonstrate skills and competencies that realistically represent problems and situations likely to be encountered in daily life. [Authentic assessment allows for] a cognitively more demanding method of assessment that has to include more discourse and reliance on emergent grammar by both the student and the instructor. (p. 5)

If classroom teachers are to allow for the construct of distributed cognition and authentic assessment methods, they need to make use of the *instructional conversations* (IC) proposed by Tharp and Gallimore (1988), who see as the role of instructors and evaluators to "allow learners to communicate beyond the a priori notions of known answers and constructs 'in the head of' the evaluator/teacher, which entails adjusting their responses to assist the speaker's cognitive efforts and language use" (p. 24). Specifically, those who assess oral proficiency must be familiar with the test-takers' second-language-learning environment, as is the case in this study, in order to provide enough opportunities for dialogue, discourse, and the co-construction of meaning through IC and methods of authentic assessment.

Douglas (2001) also provides a valuable framework, put forth by Jacoby and McNamara (1998), that includes cognition and the individual's particular field of interest or work: *indigenous assessment criteria* (IAC). Simply stated, IAC are criteria "used by subject specialists in assessing the communicative performances of apprentices in academic and vocational fields" (Douglas, 2001, p. 175) and were foreshadowed by the work of the National Language and Literacy Institute of Australia at the Language Testing Research Centre at the University of Melbourne in 1993 (Elder, 1993). The oral proficiency test, given in Italian and Japanese, served to determine the oral proficiency of future teachers of Italian and Japanese language. It also helped to certify the same teachers. As Douglas (2001) mentions, the assessment criteria were contextualized in the foreign language classroom to guide the target language use linguistically and cognitively. They did not simply assess "Italian" or "Japanese"; these tests assessed how preservice teachers interacted with their students and guided them linguistically and cognitively through tasks in the target languages.

Both Skehan (1998) and Robinson (2001) stress the importance of paying attention to cognitive factors when one addresses oral proficiency and task complexity. As the present study demonstrates, it is beneficial to the test-taker for the interviewer or tester to be familiar with each student's background, so as to provide an outline from which students can speak about their experiences. Of interest are the findings of Skehan and Foster (1999) that the more cognitively complex a task was, the more the linguistic forms deteriorated. Therefore, variation in the quality of language produced may not be the result of lack of linguistic knowledge, but rather the amount of cognitive processing necessary to successfully complete the task in the target language.

Also, rather than viewing discourse and linguistic function as being determined a priori by grammar, Hopper (1988, 1998) presents discourse as shaping grammar. In other words, it is not knowledge of a particular grammar that shapes communication or determines oral proficiency; it is the activity setting that takes into account past experiences and utterances that influences talk and dialogue (Volosinov, 1973; Mantero, 2002a). Furthermore, cognition is an adaptive and emergent process that can be readily observed during language use, as the results of this study indicate. It is the cognitive adaptation of those involved in language learning that facilitates communicative activity and the development of oral proficiency rather than the memorization of official discourse patterns and linguistic structures.

References

American Council on the Teaching of Foreign Languages (2003). *Testing for proficiency.* Retrieved January 5, 2004, from http://actfl.org

Archbald, D., & Newman, F. (1989). The functions of assessment and the nature of authentic academic achievement. In H. Berlak (Ed.), *Assessing achievement: Toward the development of a new science of educational testing* (pp. 71-84). Buffalo, NY: SUNY Press.

Bachman, L. (1990). *Fundamental considerations in language testing.* Oxford: Oxford University Press.

Bachman, L., & Savignon, S. (1986). The evaluation of communicative language proficiency: A critique of the ACTFL oral interview. *The Modern Language Journal, 70,* 380-390.

Bachman, L. F. (2000). Modern language testing at the turn of the century: Assuring that what we count counts. *Language Testing, 17,* 1-42.

Barnwell, D. (1989). Proficiency and the native speaker. *ADFL Bulletin, 20,* 2.

Bloom, B. S (1956). *Taxonomy of educational objectives: Handbook I, Cognitive domain.* New York: McKay.

Breiner-Sanders, K. E., et al. (2000). ACTFL proficiency guidelines–Speaking, revised. *Foreign Language Annals, 33,* 13-18.

Brown, A. (2003). Interviewer variation and the co-construction of speaking proficiency. *Language Testing, 20,* 1-25.

Brown, B. B. (1968). *The Florida taxonomy of cognitive behavior.* Princeton: Educational Testing Service Test Collection.

Brown, G., and Yule, G. (1983). *Discourse analysis.* Cambridge: Cambridge University Press.

Chaudron, C. (1988). *Second language classrooms: Research on teaching and learning.* Cambridge: Cambridge University Press.

Clark, J. L. D. (1972). *Foreign language testing: Theory and practice.* Philadelphia: Center for Curriculum Development.

Coulthard, M. C. (1977). *An introduction to discourse analysis.* London: Longman.

Douglas, D. (2001). Language for specific purposes assessment criteria: Where do they come from? *Language Testing, 18,* 171-185.

Elder, C. (1993). How do subject specialists construe classroom language proficiency? *Language Testing, 10,* 235-254.

Givens, C. F. (1976). A descriptive study of the cognitive level of classroom discourse of college professors and students. (Doctoral dissertation, Claremont Graduate School, 1976). *Dissertation Abstracts International, 37,* 05A.

Hagen, L. K. (1990). Logic, linguistics, and proficiency testing. *ADFL Bulletin, 21,* 2.

Hopper, P. J. (1988). Emergent grammar and the a priori grammar postulate. In D. Tannen (Ed.), *Linguistics in context: Connecting observation and understanding* (pp. 117-134). Norwood, NJ: Ablex.

Hopper, P. J. (1998). Emergent grammar. In M. Tomasello (Ed.), *The new psychology of language* (pp. 155-175). Mahwah, NJ: Lawrence Erlbaum.

Jacoby, S., & McNamara, T. (1999). Locating competence. *English for Specific Purposes, 18,* 213-241.

Johnson, K. (1995). *Understanding communication in second language classrooms.* Cambridge: Cambridge University Press.

Lantolf, J. P., & Frawley, W. (1985). Oral proficiency testing: A critical analysis. *The Modern Language Journal, 69,* 337-345.

Lantolf, J. P. (2000). *Sociocultural theory and second language learning.* Oxford: Oxford University Press.

Lincoln, Y., & Guba, E. (1985). *Naturalistic inquiry.* Beverly Hills, CA: Sage.

Liskin-Gasparro, J. E. (1984a). The ACTFL proficiency guidelines: Gateway to testing and curriculum. *Foreign Language Annals, 17,* 475-489.

Liskin-Gasparro, J. E. (1984b). *Foreign language oral proficiency testing: An organizing principle for instruction.* Paper presented at the annual meeting of the National Council on Measurement in Education. (ERIC Document Reproduction Service No. ED 263 787)

Lowe, P. (1988). The unassimilated history. In P. Lowe and C. W. Stansfield (Eds.), *Second language proficiency assessment: Current issues* (pp. 11-51). Englewood Cliffs, NJ: Prentice Hall.

Mantero, M. (2002a). *The reasons we speak: Cognition and discourse in the second language classroom.* Westport, CT: Bergin and Garvey.

Mantero, M. (2002b). Evaluating classroom communication: In support of emergent and authentic frameworks in second language assessment, *Practical Assessment, Research and Evaluation,2,* (8). Retrieved January 6, 2004, from http://pareonline.net/getvn.asp?v=8&n=8

Neisser, U. (1976). *Cognition and reality: Principles and implications of cognitive psychology.* San Francisco: Freeman.

Robinson, P. (2001). Task complexity, task difficulty, and task production: Exploring interactions in a componential framework. *Applied Linguistics, 21,* 27-57.

Savignon, S. (1972). *Communicative competence: An experiment in foreign language teaching.* Philadelphia: Center for Curriculum Development.

Skehan, P. (1998). *A cognitive approach to language learning.* Oxford: Oxford University Press.

Skehan, P., & Foster, P. (1999). The influence of task structure and processing conditions as influences on foreign language performance. *Language Learning, 49,* 93-120.

Sollenberger, H. E. (1978). Development and current use of the FSI oral interview test. In J. L. D. Clark (Ed.), *Direct testing of speaking proficiency: Theory and application* (pp. 1-12). Princeton, NJ: Educational Testing Service.

Spolsky, B. (2000). Language testing in *The Modern Language Journal*. *The Modern Language Journal, 84*, 536-552.

Tharp, R. G. , & Gallimore, R. (1988*). Rousing minds to life: Teaching, learning, and schooling in social context.* Cambridge: Cambridge University Press.

Volosinov, V. N. (1973*). Marxism and the philosophy of language.* New York: Seminar Press.

Vygotsky, L. S. (1978). *Mind in society.* Cambridge, MA: Harvard University Press.

Webb, J. N. (1970). The Florida taxonomy of cognitive behavior. In A. Simon & E. G. Boyer (Eds.), *Mirrors for behavior, an anthology of classroom observation instruments* (pp. 68-70). Philadelphia: Research for Better Schools.

Wells, G., & Claxton, G. (Eds.). (2002). *Learning for life in the 21st century.* Oxford: Blackwell.

Wiggins, G. (1990). The case for authentic assessment. *Practical Assessment, Research & Evaluation, 2* (2). Retrieved December 6, 2004, from http://pareonline.net/getvn.asp?v=2&n=2

8

Building Bridges for International Internships

Sharron Gray Abernethy
University of Alabama in Huntsville

Abstract

Most universities regard internships as key elements in the development of strong programs in foreign language and international trade education. However, it is widely recognized that a successful internship program is difficult to establish and even more difficult to sustain. This article describes the University of Alabama in Huntsville's foreign language international trade internship program and outlines the process the author used to establish it locally in year one and expand it to an international program in year two. The Business and International Education Office (BIE) of the U.S. Department of Education considers our program to be a model, and the author believes that it has value for both beginning and experienced foreign language international trade educators. The article describes the creation and development of a model that other interested educators can realistically duplicate for the benefit of their university communities.

Background

It is our belief at the University of Alabama in Huntsville (UAH) that internships are essential to the development of programs in foreign language and international trade education. Gliozzo (1999) emphasizes that international internships are increasingly significant for students to learn about America's role in today's world and that students are seeking to acquaint themselves in a practical way with opportunities available in their field of study. Recognizing that our society is part of a world system that can be explored through field-learning experiences, they want practical activities to supplement their academic work. While providing students with significant experience, well-directed internships demonstrate how foreign language and international trade education promotes market development and improved international relationships. This demonstration is particularly important in Huntsville, the largest export center in the state. The local economy is dominated by advanced technology firms in which narrowly focused technical professionals often need support from other professionals with international trade education and knowledge of foreign languages and cultures. To meet this need and create cost-effective programs, UAH's International Business Studies Initiative (IBSI), made possible through a U.S. Department of Education BIE grant, has adopted a strategy of cooperation across disciplines that is mutually beneficial to our students and to the business community. The result is a successful required international trade internship program for our department's largest degree program, Foreign Language/International Trade (FLIT). An additional benefit of our participation in the IBSI has been the opportunity afforded to us by the BIE grant to establish internship sites for *all* of our language majors (French, German, Russian, Spanish) in various key local and foreign organizations and professional offices.

Although a BIE grant afforded our institution the opportunity for a course release each semester for 2 years to allow the International Internship Coordinator to establish and implement our program, our department believes that the program can be sustained in the future and can, in fact, be established without benefit of a grant, provided that the foreign language department and the institution are committed to the goals of the program. As a result of a number of years of interaction with the local business community and service to our department as liaison to the North Alabama International Trade Association (NAITA), an organization that became our invaluable grant partner, the author collaborated with Johanna Shields, principal investigator of the grant that funded the IBSI at UAH, and became International Internship Coordinator. In addition to NAITA, the grant partnered the College of Administrative Science, the College of Liberal Arts, and the Humanities Center, resulting in the exploration and cultivation of a wealth of interdisciplinary opportunities that have benefited the university and business communities.

Internship Goals

Our syllabus states that the community provides many opportunities for students to combine their classroom study with practical work in a wide range of government, international, business, educational, and private organizations. The internship experience derived from the Foreign Language 410/International Internship class enables students with foreign language majors (French, German, Russian, or Spanish) or students with both foreign language and international trade interests (FLIT) to use their second language skills as well as to develop interdisciplinary, multicultural, and cross-cultural knowledge. Students work in an off-campus or overseas organization and meet with faculty and other students to report on their work and compare and analyze experiences. Coordinating these experiences, this course combines practical experience with discussion of ramifications of cultural diversities in the world of professions (see Appendix A).

Additional objectives of our program are to demonstrate the value of international business education for market development in local business firms and for trade relationships of local business firms. Providing internship sites gives our business community a sense of ownership in the UAH program, as well as an opportunity to observe the skills that our language students can bring to the workplace.

Establishment of the Process

Imperative to the process of identifying internship sites is the cultivation of a working relationship with local international trade organizations, the Chamber of Commerce, civic and service organizations, such as Rotary or Kiwanis, and, as in the author's case, the local chapter of Executive Women International as well. It is surprisingly easy to contact and enlist the support of the community for a worthwhile university project. These organizations seem to derive a great deal of satisfaction from providing a service to the university. In addition, most of our site providers have discovered the added benefit of receiving a valuable no-cost service to their company or organization from a well-trained student who can perform a wide variety of tasks, ranging from facilitating communication and correspondence with foreign clients to performing daily duties of the organization to helping the company explore international marketing opportunities.

In order to start the internship site search list, we enlisted the help of NAITA and Executive Women International and were able to access their list of local international businesses, complete with contact names and addresses. Officers in the organization volunteered their help in distributing questionnaires that the author designed to identify interested companies, supervisor contact information, target language interest areas, and anticipated projects or duties (see Appendix B). Additional questionnaires were circulated as leads for sites came to the author's attention. Through this process, the author was able to conduct follow-up meetings with key decision-makers of interested companies. The process resulted in 23 available internship positions, a surplus of sites for our first year's internship class of 15 students, representing all four of our target-language majors, plus one multilingual.

Simultaneously, the coordinator conducted surveys of departments of our college, as well as those of other colleges and universities that have existing internship programs, in order to glean as much information as possible about existing internship programs, UAH policies, pitfalls, recommendations, legal ramifications, and so forth. In addition, the author surveyed key NAITA members to understand what the local international businesses would expect of our students.

As a result of the survey and based on an Administrative Science recommendation, we successfully defended a highly debated proposal on behalf of the department for changing the FL 410 internship grading system from letter grade to *S/U* because of subjectivity/collaborative issues. While our faculty recognizes that a disadvantage of the pass/fail option is that it does not encourage students to excel, we believe that the nature of the FL 410 internship (the only course in our curriculum that is not entirely "academic") minimizes that disadvantage. Students entering our FL 410 are well aware that the internship is an excellent place to develop their career opportunities and are motivated to earn for their résumés a strong letter of reference from the site supervisors, recognizing as well the employment possibilities where they are serving the internships.

In the internship class there is often input from at least three people–classroom instructor/internship coordinator, site supervisor, and occasionally an additional foreign language faculty member, if the instructor's foreign language area is not that of the student. Furthermore, standards of excellence will vary from company to company and are reflected in each supervisor's expectations. Therefore, in order to receive a grade of "A," one student may have to meet much more demanding requirements than another. Acknowledging that grading systems are somewhat subjective and fallible, we diminish that impact on our students by offering FL 410 as a pass/fail course, in conformity with the internship grading policy of our College of Administrative Science and that of several other universities.

At the same time we developed a student application form that meets all UAH legal guidelines and distributed copies to professors in the department for them to distribute to students in their upper-level classes (see Appendix C). Once the forms and five copies of the required student résumés were collected, the author compiled a list of students, their majors, their specific interests, and their qualifications. The author then worked through the process of matching students' majors or interest areas with the available sites. Next came interview sessions during the early fall semester for students who were applying for the FL 410 class in the spring. Those who were not seniors were advised to postpone the internship experience until such time as they would have maximum target language ability as well as having completed most of their international-trade-related courses. It was important to glean from the students what they hoped to gain from the experience and to ensure that they were apprised of any unrealistic expectations. Afterward, the author met with immediate site supervisors to outline worthwhile duties and projects according to each student's particular interest area and major target language.

In order to administer the internship process, in addition to the site questionnaire and the student application, the author designed or adapted the following forms: (1) student internship agreement form, (2) student site evaluation form, (3) student information form, (4) form for site supervisor's evaluation of the student, (5) purpose/guidelines/procedures form, and (6) internal file form for site information. Incidentally, most established programs are willing to share their forms. The internal process required that we set up an individual file for each participating internship site, including the sites that expressed interest but did not participate in the first year, and for each student registered in FL 410.

Before the end of the fall semester, it was necessary to compile and mail to each student an information packet that included a personal letter of instruction, company contact information, an information/UAH policy notice, "Good Business Manners" brochure, "Selling Yourself at Your Job Interview" brochure, a *Planning Job Choices 2002* magazine, and the necessary legal forms. At the same time, we compiled and mailed to each site supervisor an information packet that included an introductory letter, an information brochure about our department, a Purpose/Guidelines/Procedures declaration, the assigned student's résumé, and the supervisor's evaluation form to be completed at the end of the work experience.

In each of the above packets, the author's letters confirmed student and supervisor names, phone numbers, titles, company locations, and work schedules. Both parties were reminded of their responsibilities and the dates for the established 10-week work period.

Once the work period begins, the coordinator must remain in contact with the site supervisors by means of on-site visits, teleconferences, and e-mail. Clarifications and issue resolutions are ongoing weekly responsibilities, often requiring diplomacy.

First-Year Assessments

BIE evaluators assessed the development of our internship program as a major focus of activity in the IBSI project. Gerber (2002), a BIE-appointed evaluator of the IBSI, states that in her experience, internships and study-abroad programs are generally both labor-intensive and time-consuming but are also some of the most effective vehicles for student internationalization. Based on her examination of evaluation forms from both the interns and the businesses involved, she confirms that our internship program yielded very positive results in terms of the quality of the experience. Furthermore, she states that our efforts were quite successful in identifying more internships than there were students available during the inaugural period, no small accomplishment in her assessment. Kedia (2002), our second evaluator, concludes that the IBSI has established a strong base for its internship program. After reviewing the site supervisors' evaluation forms, he reports that the evaluations ranged from very good to outstanding, and in no case did an evaluation state that the experience had been less than satisfactory. His conclusion was that UAH has made an excellent start in the area of internships.

Student site evaluations revealed that over two-thirds of the students said that the site met or exceeded their expectations. Three students, all three of whom were female Spanish majors, said that the site fell below their expectations. The fact that they were Spanish majors is probably of no significance, but the fact that they were all females led the author to investigate the possibility that college-aged females may not have had as much world-of-work experience as their male counterparts, since the first class was equally balanced with males and females. Two of the students' experiences can be explained as student/supervisor incompatibility, unrealistic expectations, and lack of previous job experience. After counseling sessions with the three female interns, the author concluded from the results of a survey of all interns that for the benefit of all participants more time needed to be spent during the formal classroom component of the FL 410 in discussions of realistic expectations in the workplace. However, an example of the situation for the third dissatisfied student was that she had been placed in a company that was acquired almost immediately thereafter by a multinational. The student observed disorganization, a frustrating situation for a beginner, and she struggled with a very unhappy, insecure supervisor. The internship coordinator concluded that such experiences would always be beyond the control of the coordinator. While an acquisition is a realistic workplace expectation, the matter was finally resolved through placement of the student at a new site. For broader assessment of the program, perhaps the most relevant question on the student evaluation form is: "What is your overall evaluation of this internship experience?" Again two-thirds of the class rated it "excellent" or "good," as opposed to "average," "fair," and "poor," thus providing very encouraging results for a first-year program.

Although there were relatively few problems associated with the first-year program, a number of learning experiences have led to more flexibility, as well as changes in the program. Initially the coordinator made an effort to vertically integrate the students' placement to the highest level possible in the large companies. A student who worked for the Director of International Programs at a large global company had an excellent experience while the director was in the country. However, such high-ranking officers in a company's international office are often out of the country and must leave students to their own initiative or under the supervision of subordinates unfamiliar with our program or the students' projects.

Other students were placed in some of our numerous high-tech international firms. A few of them became frustrated when the restrictions associated with proprietary information prevented them from getting deeply involved in worthwhile projects because of "top-secret" information to which the students could not be privy. When students did work on proprietary-related projects, some experienced problems giving the coordinator the detailed reports required weekly by the program. Some of the students' final written reports had to be screened by compliance officers before they could be submitted.

The first-year site list included companies and organizations ranging from large companies, such as a Fortune 500 company with offices in 23 countries, to small businesses seeking a share of the global market. Others ranged from a nonprofit multicultural center to the administrative office of a professional baseball team with international ties. All companies who partnered with us during this first year welcomed future participation, and all stated that the program is equally beneficial for the business and the university community. As other businesses learn about our program, the site list continues to grow.

Second-Year Goal: Internships Abroad

Our plan stated in the IBSI was to broaden and grow the internship program to our ultimate goal of providing and highly encouraging internships abroad. The intent was to start the process with the international and multinational companies who had partnered with us in the first year. Such a plan would have been much easier to institute than the one to which we had to resort. In the fall of 2002, during planning sessions with the local companies that were considered the most accessible source for sites abroad, rumors of a war with Iraq and general world political unrest led to the companies' greater fear of liability issues associated with employing a student in a foreign country. Ultimately, no company would agree to send a student to a foreign office. The coordinator was quickly reminded of Tucker's (2000) warnings of the obstacles ahead for creating international internships, to include complications of distance, time, and visa issues. He states that, although it is not impossible, the process of establishing an internship program is arduous, at best.

In addition, our own university began to discourage the process because of increased liabilities for programs abroad, especially during a time of global unrest.

We continued to counsel the students and found that the majority of them still wanted to have the experience abroad. These liabilities, including the coordinator's personal liability concerns, led to a request for more involvement from our university's Office of Legal Counsel, resulting in more legally binding student/site agreement memoranda.

With few local resources and no university funds for travel abroad, it became necessary to search for other sources for sites. Upon investigation, it was encouraging to discover that excellent viable leads for sites abroad were available through several easily accessible sources:

- Survey of students in foreign language classes to identify several foreign students whose families could provide leads for internships in their respective countries
- Survey of faculty
- International relief organizations, such as the Red Cross, that have Web sites with lists of contacts and countries where offices are located and that can provide service learning or internships
- Rotary International
- Well-established international volunteer organizations, such as Cross Cultural Solutions, found through a Web search
- One's own university's exchange programs with foreign universities
- Human resource offices of major hotel chains to locate hotels abroad that have International Group Sales offices
- Web sites on foreign product packages
- International Chamber of Commerce
- U.S. State Department
- U.S. Department of Commerce
- Embassies
- Local target-language societies, such as our city's Hispanic Society, whose members have ties to businesses and organizations in several Latin American countries
- Local churches that have projects in foreign countries
- Networking opportunities, such as attendance at conferences

Using several of these sources yielded a surplus of international sites abroad. Once lines of communication were established, there developed cultivation of relationships, with contacts abroad through letters, e-mail, and telephone. Once the site agreement was confirmed and a more personal relationship with each contact was established, further negotiations resulted in free housing or food for the interns, most of whom otherwise would not have been able to take advantage of the opportunity because of personal financial constraints. In addition, since the class credit hours and tuition remain at UAH, students were able to continue their student loans or grants, although they were working away from the university.

Examples of Summer Internships Abroad

In 2002 the task of providing internship sites abroad seemed to be an almost insurmountable challenge, given the limitations of no funds for travel abroad to develop the sites as well as the threats of war and terrorist activities. Nevertheless, building on the foundation of the successful first-year's local program and networking with local and foreign contacts resulted in our securing sites for all students who expressed an interest in going abroad. Profiles of the summer interns abroad as well as their sites follow:

- A FLIT/French major, a citizen of Turkmenistan, worked in France for approximately 6 weeks in the International Development Office at a highly respected university in Paris, under the supervision of the manager of that office. The student had free housing in the apartment of the daughter of the Associate Dean at the university and, because she was within walking distance of the university, required no local transportation during her stay.

- A FLIT/German major worked in Vienna for 6 weeks. He requested a site in the field of health care administration with a goal of developing his own company abroad. The author secured a position with the hospital administrator of Austria's largest comprehensive medical complex. He lived free in the doctors' dormitory and received one meal per day in the hospital cafeteria.

- A FLIT/Spanish major spent 4 weeks working in Costa Rica for a volunteer organization. Because she had a particular interest in conservation and ecology, she lived in a house near a rain forest with other volunteers and had the cost of her meals there included in her program fee. The student worked with orphans and senior citizens, but she also got to work a minimum of one day per week at the country's oldest and world-famous butterfly conservatory that borders the Monteverde rain forest. The conservatory ships rare species of butterflies to zoos around the world. In addition, upon my request, she took one Spanish grammar class simultaneously with the experience to strengthen her language skills.

- A FLIT/Spanish major, a citizen of Austria, completed her internship in San Juan, Puerto Rico, where she worked in the International and Group Sales Office of an international hotel, a multifacility convention center on the beach of a popular tourist area of the city. Her interest area is international hotel management. Since our university does not offer such a degree, she requested to use her language skills in that area at a site abroad. The four-star hotel provided her with one lunch per day in any of its seven restaurants. She lived in the home of the mother of a Puerto Rican government official with whom the coordinator had discussed the internship program during a BIE Directors meeting in Puerto Rico the previous summer. The student paid $50 per week for her room with breakfast and had weekend meals included.

- A finance/Spanish/German major worked in Ponce, Puerto Rico, at a coffee company under the supervision of the Vice President of Marketing and Special Projects. The author arranged for him to leave 3 weeks early for Puerto Rico and live at the home of the mother of the above-mentioned contact (at a cost of $50 plus meals, per the preceding student's agreement), where he practiced his Spanish before beginning his 6-week market study project for the coffee company. In Ponce he received at no cost use of an apartment owned by the company and only one block away from both the office and a Catholic university, where his free time was filled with rich cultural opportunities with people his age. He also received free food and a car for business and personal use.

A disappointing aspect of the program was that of seeing sites secured, only to have world politics, war, terrorist activities, and financial limitations sway students and their families to reconsider the experience abroad. Beginning in the fall, the coordinator conducted regular counseling sessions with students to explain all dangers of travel abroad. In addition, students were provided with a list of Web sites to be accessed for all travel safety considerations in specific countries. A seemingly unavoidable consequence of coordinating an internship abroad program is having students decide at the last minute not to continue with their plans to serve their internships. Profiles of those who made that decision follow:

- A Spanish major was to do volunteer work for the Red Cross in Puerto Rico, per her specific request for volunteer services. A dialogue with the Director of Volunteer Services in San Juan began the previous September to establish the site. The first contact with the director of our local organization in Huntsville was followed by the accessing of information from the international Web site. The student was to have worked in the office of the Director of Volunteer Services and was to have had a home-stay arrangement.

- A FLIT/Russian major was to spend 6 weeks in St. Petersburg, working in a paid internship at an import/export company.

- A FLIT/German major would have worked at a toy manufacturing company in Krummendorf, Germany, where she would have received an on-site free room with the possibility of a small stipend.

I mention the above specific situations to depict a realistic description of the program. Nevertheless, they contribute to the appraisal of a successful program in that these well-developed sites were made available to the students and can be cultivated for future interns.

Future of the Program

The local program continues to thrive and will always be a necessity in light of some students' inability to travel abroad because of family responsibilities, personal financial issues, or the aforementioned perils of world politics, wars, and terrorist activities that engender very real safety and liability concerns. As with any strong program, it must grow and continue to be refined. Based on student and supervisor evaluations, the spring work schedule has been extended from 10 to 12 weeks with hours increased from 8 to 10 per week for the three-credit-hour option, with less formal classroom instruction time. The six-hour credit option was added and is now very popular with students and supervisors because it allows the student to work 20 hours per week and receive more meaningful assignments as well as to gain additional work experience.

The summer mini-session was added for the same reason, as well as to accommodate the interns who went abroad during the summer. Thus the program now operates with the three- and six-credit-hour options during the spring and the summer. The local and abroad internships run concurrently during spring and summer with some administrative adjustments, such as grades of "incomplete" until the summer abroad experiences end and the final papers are submitted. Other administrative adjustments were necessary during year two, such as purging the local site list and refining the selection process, adapting the original questionnaire to fit sites abroad, adding additional counseling sessions to prepare the interns for travel abroad, and working with the UAH Office of Legal Counsel to make the student/ site agreement forms more binding.

In the second year the program grew from 15 first-year local internships to 20, with five of the interns going abroad. The coordinator is inundated with inquiries and excitement about our program from our students and those from other disciplines and universities, making the internship program an excellent recruitment tool, an advantage for all foreign language departments who struggle to recruit students. The student newspaper constantly requests updates on internship activities. Composite Student Instructional Evaluation (SIE) scores from the spring 3-hour and 6-hour groups were 96.1 and 100, respectively. The summer SIE results were 100 from each credit-hour group, both local and abroad, and all spring and summer students' in-house program evaluation forms revealed 100% satisfaction with their experience. All interns who went abroad praised the program, commenting that their experiences far surpassed their expectations. The students' final papers have become testimonials for the program. Excerpts from the final papers of the spring class of interns include comments such as these: "I have gleaned much more than a reference and a nice addition to my résumé. I have gained invaluable work experience, knowledge about the international business world, a glimpse into the workings of the workplace, and lasting memories and even friendships."[1] Another student says: "It is an invaluable experience that has definitely enriched my collegiate academic experience, and I am thankful for the opportunity that I have had."

In addition to the obvious and widely recognized enrichment that an internship abroad experience affords the foreign language student, a clear advantage of this program is that it is can be duplicated by large or small universities with or without resources. It brings university and business communities together for the betterment of both, to say nothing of the opportunities that it affords the students, many of whom have received jobs or job offers as a result of experiences that provided maximum benefit from practical work in the target culture and language. While the program depends in large part on the good will of the local and global communities, the interns *create* good will in those communities. Thus, a sustainable program that is vital for internationalizing our students and our curriculum is in place. It has attracted the attention of our entire university community, specifically our College of Liberal Arts, where several other departments have already begun to duplicate our model in recognition of the possibilities for future globalization and aware of its energizing effects on our students, faculty, staff, and partner institutions.

Notes

[1]   All interns sign an agreement to allow any part of their final papers to be quoted anonymously.

References

Gerber, L. (2002). *Evaluation of International Business Studies Initiative, Business and International Education grant project.* [unpublished external evaluation report of the IBSI program at the University of Alabama in Huntsville].

Gliozzo, C. (1999). International internships. *American Institute for Foreign Study, College Division advisors' guides.* Retrieved August 3, 1999, from http//:www.aifs.org

Kedia, B. (2002). *Evaluation of International Business Studies Initiative, Business and International Education grant project.* [unpublished external evaluation report of the IBSI program at the University of Alabama in Huntsville].

Tucker, S. (2000). Developing international relationships. In M. Ainina, S. Beaton, J. Meyer, & R. Scherer, (Eds.), *A field guide to internationalizing business education* (pp. 159-175). Austin, TX: Center for International Business Education and Research, University of Texas at Austin.

Appendix A
Syllabus for FL410, International Internship:
Comparative Languages & Cultures in Practice (3-6 Credit Hours)

Prerequisite: FL303 (or placement by examination or permission of the instructor)

Objectives:

The Huntsville area provides many opportunities for students to combine their classroom study with practical work in a wide range of government, international, business, educational, and private organizations. The internship experience derived from the Foreign Language 410 Internship class will enable students with foreign language majors (French, German, Russian, or Spanish) or students with both foreign language and international trade interests (FLIT) to use their second language skills, as well as develop interdisciplinary, multicultural, and cross-cultural knowledge. Students will work in an off-campus (or, when feasible, overseas) organization and meet with faculty and other students to report on their work and compare and analyze experiences. Coordinating these experiences, this course combines practical experience with discussion of ramifications of cultural diversities in the world of professions.

Course Schedule:

January 7:   Introduction. Internship Agreement Forms. Profile of last internship class–evaluation data/observations/recommendations. Language/culture/professions in a global context (video: "Intercultural Communicating")

January 9:   Four 20-minute lectures presenting an overview of French, German, Russian, and Hispanic culture (Drs. Gyasi, Goebel, Buksa, Abernethy), with emphasis on ramifications of cultural diversity in the professional world

January 14:   Business/Professional Etiquette (Ms. Kathy Heckman, Associate Director of Career Services, UAH) and other practical matters

January 20-April 18: Work weeks (with the exception of the week of March 24-28, Spring Break): 10 hours per week for three credit hours, or 20 hours per week for six credit hours

January 23:   Free Trade Area of the Americas Workshop, 8:30-1:30 (including lunch), Hilton Hotel, sponsored by International Business Studies Initiative (ISBI), established by a Business and International Education grant from the U.S. Department of Education and the North Alabama International Trade Association

\April 22:   Last class day–Video: "Coat of Many Countries," and class discussions relating to internship experiences/site evaluation data. Written reports due.

April 24:   Exam period–Oral presentations of written reports

Requirements:

(1)   Class attendance is imperative. Work week must consist of 10/20 hours per week. If you must be absent, you must notify your supervisor *and* your instructor, in advance if possible.

(2)   You must keep a journal of all workday activities, assignments, cross-cultural experiences, observations, etc.

(3)   Each 2 weeks you are to e-mail a report, summarizing your activities. The e-mail reports should be addressed to your supervisor *and* to your instructor, to arrive by Monday, 10:00 A.M., on the following dates for each of the previous two weeks: February 3, 17, March 3, 17, April 7, 21. *No* late report will be accepted. Note: If the need arises to discuss any sensitive or confidential issue, you are encouraged to e-mail or call me directly.

(4)   Please remember that your site evaluation form is due on April 21. You will not receive a grade without completing the report. Please put it under my door at 307 Morton Hall or give it to the secretary in the Foreign Language Office.

(5)   The final written report, due in class on April 22 *(no late report will be accepted)*, will be in essay format, approximately 4-5 pages, and will discuss the specifics of the internship experience, to include a profile of the local company/organization. Logically, the major part of your final written report should be derived from a summary of your journal. Bring one hard copy to class *and* submit a copy to me electronically as a Microsoft Word attachment.

(6)   You will present an oral summary of your report during the final examination period.

Other important dates:

Last day to withdraw with refund is January 17. Last day to withdraw is March 17. Exam period is April 24, 8:00-10:30.

Grading: Satisfactory/Unsatisfactory (Unsatisfactory counts as an "F" and will be computed in the GPA. Nonattendance or dismissal from the internship site results in an automatic "U.")

Oral/Written Report	20%
Class Discussion	15%
Interim Reports	20%
Evaluation from site supervisor	45%

Note: It is important for your instructor to be able to evaluate your work fairly and accurately in this course. It is therefore expected that for all graded assignments you will do your own work and submit your own work, unless specifically told otherwise by your instructor. See the *UAH Student Handbook* for policies relating to students' rights, responsibilities, and academic behavior. Please ask your instructor if you have questions about any of these policies or procedures. In addition, please make *every* effort not to have an "emergency" that requires you to leave the classroom once class has started.

Academic Honor Statement

I promise or affirm that I will not at any time be involved in cheating, plagiarism, fabrication, misrepresentation, or any other form of academic misconduct as outlined in the UAH Student Handbook while I am enrolled as a student at the University of Alabama in Huntsville. I understand that violating this promise will result in penalties as severe as indefinite suspension from the University of Alabama in Huntsville.

Appendix B
Questionnaire for Companies Interested in
Providing Internships to UAH Students

The Huntsville area provides many opportunities for students to combine their classroom study with practical work in a wide range of government, international, business, educational, and private organizations. The internship experience derived from the Foreign Language 410 Internship class will enable students with foreign language majors (French, German, Russian, or Spanish) or students with both foreign language and international trade interests (FLIT) to use their second language skills, as well as develop interdisciplinary, multicultural, and cross-cultural knowledge. Students will work in an off-campus (or, when feasible, overseas) organization and meet with faculty and other students to report on their work and compare and analyze experiences. Upon accepting a UAH intern at no cost to your company, you will receive the service of a well-trained student who can perform a wide variety of tasks, ranging from facilitating communication and correspondence with foreign clients to helping your company explore international marketing opportunities.

Name of Company or Organization _____

Name of Respondent _____

Telephone _____

FAX _____   E-mail _____

Would your company agree to accept a paid/unpaid intern(s) from UAH in the spring or summer of 2003 to serve in some area of international business/service learning? _____

1. Would you permit the intern(s) to work in your facility approximately 10 hours per week (12 weeks in the spring)?
   Do you prefer 40 hours per week for one month in the summer?
2. What schedule would be best for your company (two afternoons, one full day, etc.)?
3. How many internships would your company consider providing?
4. Which languages/areas would be most beneficial to your company? Please circle: French, German, Russian, Spanish, Administrative Science
   What duties would the intern perform?
5. Whom may we contact at your company to discuss the internship program?

Name _____ Title _____

Telephone _____ FAX _____ E-mail _____

6. Are you able at this time to designate a person at your company to act as a coordinator to communicate with the UAH coordinator? If so, please provide the following information:

Name _____ Title _____

Telephone _____ FAX _____ E-mail _____

Appendix C
UAH Internships
Department of Foreign Languages and Literature
Application for Spring/Summer 2004 - FL410

Name _____ Student Number _____

Class _____ Major _____ GPA _____ Graduation date _____

Citizenship: US ____   Other (specify) _____

E-mail _____ Present Address _____

Phone _____

City _____ State _____ Zip _____

Permanent Address _____ Phone _____

City _____ State _____ Zip _____

Please list the *types* of Internship/Service Learning sites that interest you most (business, health care, education, social service, media and communications, etc.):

_____

_____

When do you choose to serve your 2004 Internship?
(Circle Spring or Summer)   ___3 credits ___6 credits

Do you plan to serve your internship abroad, recognizing that the only responsibility of our program to the student is the arrangement of a site assignment? ____Yes ____No

In the event that you choose to go abroad but notify the coordinator of a change of plans later than March 1 for the summer session, it may become your responsibility to assist in locating your local site.

Please list any *specific* Internship/Service Learning sites that interest you, understanding that UAH cannot guarantee that you will receive the site of your choice:

_____

_____

Computer Languages _____
Software _____
Foreign Languages (other than your major) _____
Other Special Skills _____

To complete your application, return this completed form with 5 hard-copy résumés to the Foreign Language Office by October 1. Also e-mail a résumé as a Word attachment to < abernes@email.uah.edu>.

Authorization Statement

I, the undersigned, authorize the Foreign Language Office of the University of Alabama in Huntsville (UAH) to provide prospective internship sites or their representatives with my résumé and, if on file, my references. I understand that records will be kept of the prospective internship sites that receive my credentials and that I may have access to these records as long as my file is active.

I agree to respond promptly to all communications from the Foreign Language Office and will personally contact Dr. Sharron Abernethy if there are any changes in the information provided on this form. I will keep each interview scheduled through Dr. Abernethy or cancel the interview, in the case of an emergency, at least 24 hours in advance. I also understand that this registration form will only be viewed by the staff of the Foreign Language Department and will not be made available to prospective internship supervisors. The information I have provided on this form is true and accurate to the best of my knowledge.

Signature _____ Date _____

Board of Directors
2003-2004

2003 Advisory Board
of Sponsors & Patrons
Individual Sponsors

April Allain	Louisiana	Judi Farrelly	Louisiana
David Alley	Georgia	Sylviane Finck	Louisiana
Sheree Altmann	Georgia	Terry Finlay	Georgia
Cherry Andrews	Alabama	Linda Frazier	North Carolina
Laura Arguea	Florida	Howard Furnas	Alabama
Corinne Barnes	Georgia	Pamela Gay	Alabama
Sue Barry	Alabama	Monique Glover	Georgia
John Bartley	Georgia	Otmara González	Georgia
Mitzi Bayne	Georgia	Kenneth Gordon	Missouri
Amy Benson	Alabama	Jane Govoni	Florida
Ginger Biggs	Louisiana	Esperanza Granados	South Carolina
Melissa Blancaneaux	Louisiana	John Green	Georgia
Evelyne Bornier	Louisiana	Scott Grubbs	Georgia
Janice Boyles	South Carolina	Jo Anna Hallman	Florida
Lee Bradley	Georgia	Julia Hanley	Georgia
Evelyn Brady	Georgia	Karen Harrell	Alabama
Linda Braun Font	Georgia	Betty Hickox	Georgia
Jacqueline Bravelaway	Alabama	Jean Hicks	Alabama
Elisa Brown	Georgia	Lola Hidalgo-Calle	Florida
Lynn Brown	Florida	Kay Hoag	South Carolina
Michele Brown	Tennessee	Marianna Holloman	South Carolina
Vitalia Bryn-Pundyk	Arkansas	Mary Jim Howe	South Carolina
Christia Burgess	South Carolina	Sandra Hunt	Georgia
Laura Campagna	Louisiana	Shirley Hurd	South Carolina
Patricia Carlin	Arkansas	Maria Jackson	Alabama
Marilyn Carpenter	West Virginia	David Jahner	Georgia
Rosalie Cheatham	Arkansas	Dorie Johansen	South Carolina
Sharon Cherry	South Carolina	Marsha Johnson	South Carolina
Jim Chesnut	Georgia	Lucia Jones	Georgia
Jeanne Classé	Alabama	Norah Jones	Virginia
Kay Clements	Alabama	Maria Jovanovich	Florida
Cassandra Connolly	Georgia	Glenna Kappel	Florida
Judith Cox	Alabama	Kim Kappel	Florida
Joanna Crane	Alabama	Caroline Kelly	North Carolina
Melissa Damerson-Vines	Alabama	Chad Kison	Alabama
Catherine Danielou	Alabama	Jacqueline Konan	Georgia
Jean-Louis Dassier	Michigan	Lizette Laughlin	South Carolina
Nancy De Young	South Carolina	Alison Leininger	Alabama
Michael Dockery	Georgia	Ally Leonard	Alabama
Daphne Eidson	Georgia	Melanie Lewis	Louisiana
Penny Evans	Georgia	Keith Lindley	Alabama
Leila Falt	Alabama	Lin Lindsay	Georgia
Valerie Farlow	Georgia	Mark Linsky	Georgia

Name	State
Heidi Lomangino	Alabama
Sheri Long	Alabama
María López	Georgia
Ines Lormand	Louisiana
Candi Love	South Carolina
Jill Mange	Alabama
Judith Martin	Florida
Leigh Martin	Alabama
Elaine McAllister	Georgia
Lynne McClendon	Georgia
Sharon McClure	Alabama
Shelia McCoy	Georgia
Alissa McDonough	Georgia
Mary McGehee	Louisiana
Lisa Melendez	Georgia
Carlos Mentley	South Carolina
Cindy Metty	South Carolina
Pam Middlebrooks	Georgia
Nidza Miller	Alabama
Tatiana Milton	Louisiana
Peter Meister	Alabama
Sarah Meister	Alabama
Mazie Movassaghi	Louisiana
Susan Murphy	South Carolina
Candace Nanista	Georgia
Helen Newton	South Carolina
Anne Nietert	South Carolina
Pat Nix	Alabama
Kathryn Norman	Mississippi
Nancy Norris	North Carolina
Mary Oestriecher	Louisiana
Mario Ortiz	Mississippi
Karen Palmer	Louisiana
Linda Paragone	Alabama
Janet Parker	Virginia
Francisco Romero Pérez	S.Carolina
Amelia Perry	Alabama
Leslie Pourreau	Georgia
Sandra Preston	Florida
Mark Putnam	Florida
Sharon Rapp	Arkansas
Rachel Reed	South Carolina
Lucinda Rivera	Georgia
Aileen M. Robertson	Louisiana
Cathy Robison	South Carolina
Peter Rosborough	Alabama
Sue Ross	Alabama
Pilar Rus	South Carolina
Jennifer Russell	Florida
Tatum Saltz	Alabama
Jean Santini	Alabama
Richard Sayers	Colorado
Tricia Schryer	Alabama
Rosalba Scott	North Carolina
Brian Shedd	Georgia
David Shook	Georgia
Lisa Signori	South Carolina
Lynn Simmons	Georgia
Margit Sinka	South Carolina
Carol Skidmore	Alabama
Faye Smith	Alabama
Robin Snyder	West Virginia
Samia Spencer	Alabama
Marcia Spielberger	Georgia
Edwina Spodark	Virginia
Jonita Stepp-Greany	Florida
Clarita Stone	Alabama
Mary Stovall	Alabama
Alice Strange	Missouri
Janene Sullivan	Georgia
Maxine Taylor	Georgia
Robert Terry	Virginia
Carmen Tesser	Georgia
Nellie Tietz	Alabama
Alfred Treviño	Virginia
Estela Treviño	Virginia
Deborah Tucker	Tennessee
Mary-Elizabeth Via	Virginia
Maria Villadoniga	Florida
Jeanne Walker	Georgia
Nancy Wall	Alabama
Frances Weathers	Mississippi
Nadine Wells	North Carolina
Jonathan Whitfield	South Carolina
Lee Wilberschied	Ohio
Carol Wilkerson	Tennessee
Andrea Wilkinson	Alabama
Janet Williams	Georgia
John D. Williams	Georgia
Jennifer Winburn	Tennessee
Jerry Winfield	Georgia
Terri Wittmeier	Alabama
Marcia Woodward	South Carolina

2003 Advisory Board of
Sponsors & Patrons
Representing Institutions and Organizations

Alliance Française de Mobile (Mobile, AL)
>   Colette Windish
American Association of Teachers of German (AATG)
>   Helene Zimmer Loew
Atlanta Public Schools (Atlanta, GA)
>   Deborah Reidmiller
Augusta State University (Augusta, GA)
>   Jana Sandarg and Mary Kathleen Blanchard
Belmont University (Nashville, TN)
>   Cheryl Brown and David Julseth
Cemanahuac Educational Community
>   Vivian Harvey
Central States Conference on Language Teaching (CSC)
>   Patrick Raven
Clarke County High School (Grove Hill, AL)
>   Lois Davis
Consulat Général de France d'Atlanta
>   Cecile Peryonnet and Aurelien Lepine-Kousas
Father Ryan High School (Nashville, TN)
>   Laura Beasley
Florida Foreign Language Association (FFLA)
>   Louis Lillard
Foreign Language Association of Virginia (FLAVA)
>   Valerie Gooss
Furman University (Greenville, SC)
>   Maurice Cherry
Georgia Chapter of the American Association of Teachers of French
>   Dina Foster and David de Posada
Georgia College and State University (Milledgeville, GA)
>   Roger Noël
Georgia Department of Education (Atlanta, GA)
>   Elizabeth Webb
Georgia Education Office of Spain (Atlanta, GA)
>   Vicente Valverde

Georgia Southern University (Statesboro, GA)
    Clara Krug and Horst Kurz
Grant County High School (Dry Ridge, KY)
    Chelo Díaz Martín
Gray Middle School (Union, KY)
    Luis García
Holy Innocents' Episcopal School (Marietta, GA)
    Anne Jackson
Howard University (Forestville, MD)
    Herman Bostick
Interprep (Marietta, GA)
    Greg Duncan
Kentucky State Department of Education (Frankfort, KY)
    Jacque Bott Van Houten
Louisiana State Department of Education (Baton Rouge, LA)
    Carolyn Taylor-Ward
Macon State University (Macon, GA)
    Lynn Bryan and David de Posada
Mount St. Mary Academy (Little Rock, AR)
    Sue Mistic and Maureen Stover
Mountain Brook Jr. High School (Mountain Brook, AL)
    George Ann Parker
National FLES* Institute
    Gladys Lipton
North Carolina State University (Raleigh, NC)
    Susan Navey-Davis
Northeast Conference on the Teaching of Foreign Languages (NECTFL)
    Rebecca Kline
Pacific Northwest Council for Languages
    Teresa Kennedy
Paulding County School District (Dallas, GA)
    Maureen Clouse
Prattville High School (Prattville, AL)
    Emilia Chávez Saphore and Marlin Harris
Randolph School (Huntsville, AL)
    Peggy Bilbro, Glynn Below, Vally Perry, Francoise Wackenhut
Samford University (Birmingham, AL)
    Myralyn Allgood
Shades Valley High School (Irondale, AL)
    Phyllis Clay
Shelby County Schools (AL)
    Janet Smith
South Carolina Department of Education
    Ruta Couet

South Carolina Foreign Language Teachers' Association (SCFLTA)
        Luana Coleman and Lynn Fulton-Archer
Southwest Conference on Language Teaching (SWCOLT)
        Audrey Cournia
Tennessee Chapter, American Association of Teachers of Spanish and Portuguese
        Deb Lamine and Dorothy Winkles
The Language House (Greenville, SC)
        Nardina Alongi
Université du Québec à Chicoutimi
        Pierre Lincourt
University of Central Florida (Tampa, FL)
        Karen Verkler
University of South Carolina (Spanish and Portuguese)
        Carolyn Hansen and David Hill
University of the South (Sewanee, TN)
        Jim Davidheiser
Valdosta State University (Valdosta, GA)
        Ellen Friedrich and Amy Aronson-Friedman
West Virginia University (Morgantown, WV)
        Maria Amores, Sharon Wilkinson, Frank Medley (Emeritus)
West Virginia State Department of Education (Charleston, WV)
        Deborah Harki

Joel Walz   Personalizing FL Instruction with
                                           World Wide Web Home Pages

Leona B. LeBlanc   The Use of Writing Assistant Software: An
     and Rebecca L. Chism   Effective Tool in Improving Writing?

Daniel MacDougall   Connecting Content Areas Via Music
                                        in the Elementary FL Class

Carolyn Lally   Using the National Standards to Improve FL
                       Articulation: An Alternative to Placement Exams

Addressing the Standards for
Foreign Language Learning: Dimension '97

Marjorie H. DeWert   Developing Tomorrow's
     and Audrey Heining-Boynton   Technology-Using FL Teachers

Leona LeBlanc   FL Placement in Postsecondary
     and Carolyn G. Lally   Institutions

Sheri Spaine Long   Pedagogy and the Emerging Spanish Canon

Alice J. Strange   A French Culture Course in English:
                                     Strategies and Resources

Yoshihiro Tajima   A Task-Based Communicative
     and Hiroko Spees   Approach in FLES

Ellen Lorraine Friedrich, Lollie Barbare   Strategies in Recruiting and
     Eykyn, and Barbara Owens McKeithan   Retaining Students in
                                                          French Classes

Charlotte Blackmon   Small World Language and Culture for
     and Lorene Pagcaliwagan   Children: FLEX and the New Standards

---

Volumes for 2004 and 2003 are available for purchase at $10 each.
Previous volumes of ***Dimension*** are available for purchase at $5.00 each.

EIN 23-7027288

SCOLT Publications
1165 University Center
Valdosta State University
Valdosta, GA 31698

Telephone 229 333 7358   http://www.valdosta.edu/scolt/
Fax 229 333 7389   Lbradley@valdosta.edu